JAPANESE BUSINESS LAW AND THE LEGAL SYSTEM

Recent Titles from QUORUM BOOKS

Pension Fund Investments in Real Estate: A Guide for Plan Sponsors and Real Estate Professionals
Natalie A. McKelvy

Growth Industries in the 1980s: Conference Proceedings
Federal Reserve Bank of Atlanta, Sponsor

Business Strategy for the Political Arena
Frank Shipper and Marianne M. Jennings

Socio-Economic Accounting
Ahmed Belkaoui

Corporate Spin-Offs: Strategy for the 1980s
Ronald J. Kudla and Thomas H. McInish

Disaster Management: Warning Response and Community Relocation
Ronald W. Perry and Alvin H. Mushkatel

The Savings and Loan Industry: Current Problems and Possible Solutions
Walter J. Woerheide

Mechatronics
Mick McLean, Editor

Establishing and Building Employee Assistance Programs
Donald W. Myers

The Adversary Economy: Business Responses to Changing Government Requirements
Alfred A. Marcus

Microeconomic Concepts for Attorneys: A Reference Guide
Wayne C. Curtis

Beyond Dumping: New Strategies for Controlling Toxic Contamination
Bruce Piasecki, Editor

Payments in the Financial Services Industry of the 1980s: Conference Proceedings
Federal Reserve Bank of Atlanta, Sponsor

JAPANESE BUSINESS LAW AND THE LEGAL SYSTEM

Elliott J. Hahn

QUORUM BOOKS
Westport, Connecticut
London, England

Library of Congress Cataloging in Publication Data

Hahn, Elliott J.
  Japanese business law and the legal system.

  Bibliography: p.
  Includes index.
  1. Commercial law—Japan. 2. Industrial laws and
legislation—Japan. I. Title.
LAW   346.52'07   84-3276
ISBN 0-89930-047-2 (lib. bdg.) 345.2067

Library of Congress Catalog Card Number: 84-3276
ISBN 0-89930-047-2

First published in 1984 by Quorum Books

Greenwood Press
A division of Congressional Information Service, Inc.
88 Post Road West, Westport, Connecticut 06881

Printed in the United States of America

10 9 8 7 6 5 4 3 2 1

Copyright Acknowledgments

Grateful acknowledgment is given for permission to use the following:
"An Overview of the Japanese Legal System," Elliott J. Hahn, *Northwestern Journal of International Law & Business* 517 (1983), appears here as chapter 2 in slightly revised form with the permission of the *Journal.*
Excerpts from "Negotiating with the Japanese," Elliott Hahn, 2 *The California Lawyer,* (March 1982), with the permission of the publisher.
Excerpts from "Japanese Fee Practice," *International Lawyers' Newsletter* 1, July/August 1981.
Excerpt from "Fractured Japanese," David Tharp, *The Japan Times,* June 14, 1980.
Figure 4, taken from "The Changing Role of Japan's General Traders," Thomas Cappiello, *Tradepia International* 12, Autumn 1982.
McDonald's Trademark reproduced with registration symbol with the permission of McDonald's Corporation.

To my parents—for their love and support

Contents

Figures

Tables

Acknowledgments

The idea for this book originated with my teaching of courses on Japanese business law and the legal system of Japan at California Western School of Law in San Diego and in the Santa Clara Law School Summer in Tokyo Program. In response to requests from both my students and Western businessmen and attorneys who do business with Japan and the Japanese, I sought to find one book that was an overview of Japan's business law and legal system. Increasingly frustrated by my failure to find such a book, I put together the materials that form the basis of this book.

Many people have helped me during the writing of this work. The arguments advanced, the conclusions reached, and any errors are, though, solely my own. In particular, I would like to thank the Haraguchi family, Bradley Ware, Professors Phil Jimenez and Richard Rykoff of Santa Clara Law School, Glen Krebs, the Nakamura family, and the students, faculty, and staff at California Western for all of their help and advice. Robert Brown deserves special thanks for his many incisive comments about the Japanese legal system; in addition, he has always been very generous with his time and help. Professors Julius Cohen and Ved Nanda were kind enough to read parts of the manuscript and offer comments. Thanks also go to Professor Keizo Sakata (all Japanese names in this work are cited in the Western way, i.e., family name last) of Nihon University in Tokyo and the staff and faculty at that school for furnishing me with an office and supplies in the summer of 1982 to work on this book. Lynn Taylor of Greenwood Press has given me constant help whenever asked, and Marcia Greenberg of the *Northwestern Journal of International Law and Business* gave me insightful comments about Chapter 2 (which was printed in that periodical as an excerpt from this work). My thanks also go to *The California Lawyer*, the journal of the California bar, for allowing me to use part of the material from my article on "Negotiating with the Japanese" (published in the March of 1982 issue) in this book. My student assistants Quinn Hunsaker, Paul Nussbaum, Joanne Bradley and Sue Pess furnished valuable research assistance. Jane Morley, Marilyn Masterson, and especially Mary-Ellen Norvell of the California Western faculty secretarial staff showed the utmost of patience during a long process of writing, revising, and updating. Finally, special thanks go to my dear friend Kuniharu Yasue, an attorney in Tokyo. During the 1982 and 1983 summers he took time from a very busy schedule both to introduce me to people in Japan who might be of help to me in my research and to accompany me to speak with others. I owe him a great deal, and I thank him. Special thanks also go to his many friends in Tokyo who did not hesitate to give me whatever help they could. To all of the people named, and to all the others who helped, I give my thanks.

JAPANESE
BUSINESS LAW
AND THE
LEGAL SYSTEM

Introduction   1

Despite the seemingly ubiquitous presence of Japan in the media today, widespread misperceptions of that nation abound in America. These misperceptions, ones caused by both omissions of information and erroneous statements, cause us obvious problems. As the importance of Japan to the United States has grown in recent years in seemingly direct proportion to the rise in Japan's economic power, so have these problems seemed to increase at a corresponding rate. According to one prominent Japanese official, "Western ignorance of Japan has now become an extremely serious problem."[1]

Many Americans who negotiate and do business with the Japanese, and others who are interested in the process, encounter problems because they do not see the differences between the business law systems of Japan and the United States. Others encounter difficulties because they perceive differences, some overt and some subtle, between the two systems, but they do not understand them. Perhaps the most frustrating situation is that of the Americans who do business in Japan and understand many of the differences between the two business law systems—but either fail to recognize the others or misunderstand them. In any case, though, these non-perceptions and misunderstandings have caused ill-formed decisions to be made with a subsequent lack of success for many American companies in Japan. Obviously, many of these problems would not have occurred if the Americans involved had a better understanding of the Japanese business law system. The problems caused by these non-perceptions and misunderstandings can become so frustrating as to cause American companies to close their businesses in Japan. Others, discouraged by the differences in the business law systems of the two nations, have decided not to do business in Japan in the first place. To decide, however, not to do business in Japan can be a very costly decision; one must literally be a hermit today not to realize how incredibly potent is the Japanese market (see figure 1.1

FIGURE 1.1

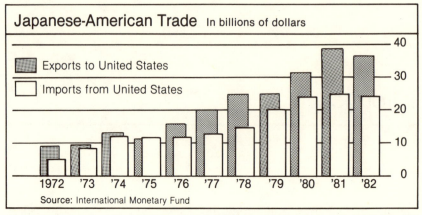

"Japan to Strengthen Yen, Cut Tarriffs," *Los Angeles Times,* October 21, 1983, Part IV ("Business"), at 1.

demonstrating the growth of U.S.-Japanese trade). That island-nation of 110 million people has a gross national product whose growth since 1950 can only be described as "awesome."[2] Japan is the free world's second largest market. Its 1981 g.n.p. of $1,127 billion was almost double that of West Germany and equal to the combined g.n.p.'s of France and Britain.[3] Japan is one of the principal growth machines not just in the Asia-Pacific region but in the world. By the end of this century, according to World Bank projections, Japan's g.n.p. is expected to be equal to three-quarters of that of the United States (compared with about one-half at present) while her citizens will enjoy a per capita income considerably higher than that of Americans.[4]

The basic tenet that must be kept in mind by Occidentals at all times is that for all of its Western veneer, underneath the surface Japan is a far different place than any Western nation. In their rules, customs, and values the Japanese are like no other people. Yet many Americans on their visits to Japan see only the modern department stores, the Western dress, the many cameras, televisions, and radios, and the apparent facility with which many Japanese speak English—all of these factors leading the Americans to conclude that "the Japanese are just like us." That statement is not only wrong but also dangerous; the American who believes in its veracity will encounter serious roadblocks, if not insurmountable obstacles, in his attempt to achieve a successful business relationship with the Japanese. One American was recently quoted as saying: "Somebody comes here from the United States and he sees those modern buildings and all the Japanese in suits and ties and he thinks he's back in California.... But it would be a lot more accurate if the Japanese he met shaved their heads, wore kimonos, and carried swords to meetings. It's that different here."[5]

An American must not only be aware of how different the Japanese are but also be careful not to judge and evaluate all he observes by his own values. The American who brings into his business dealings with the Japanese fixed Western cultural and sociological values and ideas that have been imprinted on him through his rearing, education, and life in the West will most likely not achieve the results he desires. Although in large part the company has today replaced the role the village group once held in Japan, still Japan is a country whose people have continued to maintain beliefs that marked the country for centuries even before it was opened to the West by the historic entrance of Admiral Matthew Calbraith Perry into Shimoda Bay in 1853. In dealing with the Japanese, the American lawyer or businessman must not only take obvious precautions to see that the laws of the two nations are taken into account in the negotiation, drafting, execution, and performance of the contract—but also, just as importantly, make sure that through ignorance or lack of attentiveness he does not displease or even anger the Japanese by transgressing on a strongly held value of theirs and thus possibly jeopardize the business relationship of the parties. The Japanese are a very different people with far different values and customs. Whether or not the American likes these ways is one matter; surely, though, to have a successful business relationship with the Japanese, he must be cognizant and respectful of them.

The purpose of this book is to give American lawyers and businessmen an overview of the Japanese business law system so that they can better prepare for negotiating with the Japanese, better plan in what way they wish to enter the Japanese market, and be more familiar with events that may occur once they are doing business there. It is my hope in writing this book that the reader will not only gain a stronger understanding of the Japanese business law system but also that he will be better able to understand the Japanese with whom he is dealing. Thus, many of the points covered in this book will not be strictly legal per se; it is my strongly held belief that a person discussing the Japanese business law system would be remiss if he did not mention the cultural, sociological, and economic beliefs behind it. Indeed, the American consulting firm Arthur D. Little, Inc., concluded a few years ago that "for American business in Japan the most fundamental and pervasive obstacles to exporting are those structural characteristics of Japanese society which we have called cultural and business practices."[6]

The uniqueness of this book is that it is written for both the lawyer and the businessman who wish to learn more about the Japanese business law system. Although there have been in the last few years many works written on this subject as the specter of the Japanese economy has loomed larger and larger in the American consciousness, virtually all have been written on the intricacies of the Japanese economy. Few have been written on the legal aspects; of those that have been written on this subject, most of them are general works with little attention paid to the nuances of the Japanese business law system. This book is an effort to synthesize the needs of the two groups and to explain the Japanese business law system. The purpose of this book is not, in effect, to write a treatise on the workings of the Japanese business law system. Rather, it is intended to be a primer on the workings of the Japanese business law system for the American lawyer or businessman who needs to understand the major aspects of the system and how to work within it—or obviously for anyone else who may be interested in an overview of the Japanese business law system. It is my earnest hope that the material in this book will be of practical value to Americans in the future; not only are more and more Japanese businesses being started in the United States but at the same time the American pressure on the Japanese to open their borders to American goods and investments is having an effect, albeit a gradual one, so that the opportunities for American businesses in Japan are increasing at a steady rate.[7] Just as earnestly, however, I hope that this book will prove to be of value to more Americans than just those who are involved in business dealings with the Japanese. In my opinion, no relationship with an ally is more crucial to the United States than the one it has with Japan; recently, such august personages as Mike Mansfield have made public statements to the same effect. Thus, it is critical to our future that we understand the workings of the Japanese system. The greater our knowledge and the fewer the misunderstandings between our two peoples, the stronger our relationship will be.

The topic encompassed by this book is obviously a large and complex one. This work does not pretend to cover completely the Japanese business law system. Instead, I have tried to take the major areas and discuss the points of which an American should be aware in his business dealings with the Japanese. It should be kept in mind, however, that many of the points made concerning the customs and values of the Japanese are general ones; the nuances of each may differ depending on the individual Japanese involved. Hopefully, this book will give the reader a greater sensitivity to the Japanese business law system and to the beliefs, customs, modes of behavior, and values of those within it. Only by possessing such a sensitivity can the American involved achieve a business relationship with the Japanese that will benefit both sides.

NOTES

1. Watanabe, "E.T. Too Brutal," 1 *Journal of Japanese Trade and Industry* 5 (September 1982).

2. From the ashes of her defeat in World War II, Japan has experienced a

phenomenal economic growth. The gross national product of Japan in 1981 was about $1,127 billion dollars (based on an exchange rate of ¥260 to $1), the third highest g.n.p. in the world and the second in the free world. This information was obtained on September 2, 1982, by telephone from Melanie Humphrey, a staff assistant at the Japan Economic Institute in Washington, D.C.

3. Yamashita, "The Stakes and the Statistics," 2 *Journal of Japanese Trade and Industry* 23 (March/April 1983).

4. *See* Derek Davies, "Community Begins at Home," *Far Eastern Economic Review*, December 10, 1982, at 67, 68-69.

5. "The Japanese Tactic of Killing with Silence," *Far Eastern Economic Review*, June 11, 1982, at 57.

6. Arthur D. Little, Inc., *The Japanese Non-Tariff Trade Barrier Issue: American Views and the Implications for Japan-U.S. Trade Relations IV* 32 (1979).

7. At the end of 1981, for example, the Japanese had a controlling interest in over 210 U.S. manufacturing companies alone. S. MacKnight, *Japan's Expanding Manufacturing Presence in the United States: A Profile* 2 (1981). By the end of 1983 the number had expanded to 309 (not including the 25 in which Japanese parent companies have minority interests), 15A *Japan Economic Institute Report* 1 (April 13, 1984).

Lawyers, Legal Education, Quasi-Lawyers, and the Court System of Japan   **2**

Even before the beginning of what most historians term "modern" Japan, i.e., the Meiji Era in 1868,[1] Japan had developed a commercial law system, one based almost entirely on custom. Despite the influence of traditional Chinese law on other areas of its legal system, such as public and criminal law, Japan's commercial law system was almost entirely indigenous.[2] These customs were known and used by the commercial society of Japan, and, when a problem did arise, the commercial customs were enforced by various self-regulatory guilds and trade associations and, ultimately, by the courts.[3]

There were no lawyers per se in Japan, at least as we in the United States use this term, before the Meiji Era.[4] Nor was there any type of specialized legal training to instruct people in counseling others or in representing them in court. In fact, the legal and political systems acting in concert with the social values of Japan exerted a strong, virtually overwhelming, pressure on the people to resolve their problems by themselves without the aid of a third party. The Tokugawa governments (1603-1868)[5] adopted Confucianism and its doctrines of social hierarchy and "wa" (harmony) as a state orthodoxy in an effort to prevent commercial disputes from reaching any type of formal stage. Confucianism emphasizes the duty of people to serve their superiors and the duty of all in society to maintain social harmony; the Tokugawa system took these tenets and used them as societal pressures to force potential litigants to settle their problems by themselves, refrain from litigation, and thus preserve the harmony of society. Litigation to pursue one's individual rights was strongly discouraged by the system. To attempt to press one's rights in courts was seen as a disruption of the

This chapter by the author was previously published in slightly revised form in 5 *Northwestern Journal of International Law & Business*, 517 (1983), and is used with permission.

societal harmony so strongly emphasized by Confucianism. To have one's rights emphasized in court meant that another had to be told that he had erred. The Tokugawa system abhorred such judgments. Conciliation was the dominant feature, in fact, of civil procedure in the Tokugawa period.[6] Societal harmony was the all-important objective. The rights of the individual mattered little. The concept of individual rights was, in fact, so alien to the Japanese of the Tokugawa era that they had no word or phrase to express the idea. The Japanese could not envision one having rights against the state itself.[7]

Although at first glance a vestige of an earlier age, the Tokugawa society's emphasis on the settlement of disputes by the parties themselves without resort to litigation has important ramifications today. This traditional precept is still held by many Japanese. As a result, the American who wishes to have a successful long-term business relationship with the Japanese must put aside his Western law-oriented emphasis on the rights and duties of the parties as delineated by the contract. To the Japanese, determining whose rights are at stake in a dispute is not nearly as important as preserving the "wa," the harmony, between the parties. Whereas Americans resolve a dispute by looking to the language of the contract itself to see how the rights and duties of the parties are defined, many Japanese consider the language of the contract to be secondary to the spirit of trust that exists between the parties. The Japanese believe that the parties should work out problems amicably in a spirit of trust and cooperation, often regardless of what the contract says and sometimes even in the very face of the contractual language.

Traditional Japanese contracts are strange animals indeed, to American lawyers. These documents are short (often one page) recitals of the parties' rights and obligations in which the parties broadly agree to negotiate in good faith any problem that may arise.[8] Just as in the Tokugawa era the rights of the individual mattered little when balanced against the disruption to the harmony of society caused by his litigation, so analogously today many Japanese still believe that the vindication of one's rights in a contract dispute is not nearly as important as the rending of the atmosphere of trust in the business relationship caused by the pressing of one's rights. The emphasis hence becomes a negotiation of the dispute in a spirit of harmony to ensure that the atmosphere of trust is maintained. Individual rights of the parties in business relations are sacrificed so that the harmony inherent in a successful business relationship between parties is continued and even strengthened.

It should be noted, however, that the larger Japanese companies (such as Mitsui, Mitsubishi, Sumitomo, etc.) have "learned" from their American counterparts how important contractual language is in defining the duties of the parties. The Japanese have changed somewhat in international contracts. They have moved from their traditional reliance on wa and the relegation of the contract language to a secondary role to another view, a more Western one. Nevertheless, the Tokugawa/ Confucian emphasis on wa, trust, and internal resolution of their problems by the parties themselves remains a crucial factor in maintaining a strong business relationship with the Japanese.[9] The American who at the first sight of trouble threatens litigation will be shunned by the Japanese. Instead, if he values his relationship with the Japanese, he must work to resolve the matter in a spirit of amicability and trust. If a literal reading of the contract's language will result in confrontation between the parties, the Japanese will compromise the goal.[10] The Japanese view a business relationship between parties as an area where cooperation should be the goal, not conflict over the rights and duties of the parties.

After the Meiji Restoration in 1868, the new government of Japan took steps to import a Western law system into Japan. This action was taken to end the onus on Japan of two treaties imposed upon the country by the Western nations. The treaties put Japan in an inferior position to the Western nations and were considered by the Japanese to be a slur upon the country's sovereignty. One treaty dealt with customs and duties and imposed high tariffs on Japanese goods imported by the West while imposing low tariffs on Japanese imports of Western goods.[11] The other provided that because of Japan's "barbaric" legal system Westerners accused of crimes in Japan would be tried not in Japan but in their home country; as a result, the worst penalty usually imposed on a foreigner was literally a slap on the wrist.[12] When Japanese leaders asked the Western nations how these two treaties could be changed, they were told that one task they needed to accomplish was to adopt a "modern" (i.e., Western) legal system. Consequently, Japanese scholars journeyed to France, Germany, England, and the United States to determine which system should be the model for Japan. In the end, the Western legal system most heavily influencing Japan's model was the civil law system of Germany.[13]

After World War II, the legal system of the United States exerted a strong influence on Japan. Her current Constitution, put into effect in 1947, reflects a strong American influence. The Japanese corporate, civil rights, securities regulation, income tax, and labor laws also carry strong overtones of the law of the United States, as did her antitrust laws for an initial period after 1945. Thus, today the Japanese commercial legal system constitutes a unique hybrid of a civil law (Germany) and common law (U.S.A.) system grafted onto a legal system based on the customs and values that have existed in Japan for hundreds of years.

In analyzing the Japanese business law system today, one is struck by the paucity of attorneys there. Japan has roughly 12,000 lawyers, while her population is about 117 million. There are more lawyers than that just in California, a place with one-fifth of Japan's population. The United States has twice as many people as Japan and fifty times as many lawyers.[14] There is in the United States one attorney per 515 people; in Japan there is one attorney per 9,622 persons.[15]

The main reason why Japan has so few lawyers is that there is only one law school in the entire country: the Legal Training and Research Institute, located in Tokyo. To be admitted to the practice of law in Japan, one must graduate from that school.[16] A unique feature of the Institute is that its students are considered employees of the Ministry of Justice. As such, they receive a salary paid by the government during their time of study there.[17] The high intelligence of Japan's attorneys is easily inferred from the statistic that the Institute accepts less than 2 percent of those who apply for admission each year. In 1983, for example, roughly 30,000 Japanese took its entrance examination and only about 500 were admitted, a figure that is normal for the Institute.[18] The exam itself is only given once a year; failure to pass it, however, does not preclude one from taking it the next time.[19] The average entrant into the Institute, in fact, does not pass the exam until five years after graduating from college.[20]

The examination for entrance to the Legal Training and Research Institute is composed of four different parts. The first tests the applicant's general knowledge. If the applicant is a college graduate, he is exempt from that part of the test. The second, third, and fourth parts of the examination all test legal knowledge. The first and second parts of the examination are multiple-choice, the third essay, and the fourth oral.

The examination to enter the Legal Training and Research Institute is open only to the Japanese. Article 4 of the Bengoshi Ho (Lawyers' Law) is the governing statute; it states that "any person who has completed the course of study at the Legal Training and Research Institute shall be competent to practice as a lawyer." At first glance, this law seems to allow non-Japanese to be admitted to practice law in Japan, as long as they graduate from the Legal Training and Research Institute. In 1955, however, the Japanese Supreme Court restricted admission to the school to Japanese only.[21] The Court declared that since those who attend the school receive a salary from the government, they are also employees of the Ministry of Justice; only Japanese citizens can be so employed. In at least one instance since then, the Supreme Court did allow a non-Japanese to attend the school. That case, though, was a unique one involving a Korean named Kyeong Deuk Kim who had been born and raised in Japan, whose family had lived in Japan for several generations, but who was still considered by the Japanese to be a Korean (under Japanese law one's nationality is determined

not by country of birth but by the nationality of one's father).[22] In light
of strong pressure from the bar, since he had been born, raised, and
educated in Japan, and because he lived in Japan, the Supreme Court
in 1977 permitted him to enter the Institute. In 1979, the Supreme
Court did amend the admission requirements of the Legal Training
and Research Institute to provide that foreigners in "appropriate" cases
may be admitted. Apparently, however, no such appropriate case has
yet been found. To my knowledge, no foreigner has been admitted to
the Legal Training and Research Institute since that date; certainly,
no American has.

Since the Legal Training and Research Institute is the sole source
of lawyers in Japan, the closest analogue to the American bar
examination is the test to enter the Institute. A major difference between
the two legal systems is therefore that in the United States each
jurisdiction administers a bar examination to those who have graduated
from law school and wish to practice law in that jurisdiction. In contrast,
in Japan the bar examination is actually a test given before one enters
law school, i.e., it is the entrance examination for the Legal Training
and Research Institute.[23] Since there is only one law school in Japan,
the key examination thus becomes not the one to graduate from the
school but rather the one to qualify for admission. In this way Japan
severely limits the number of attorneys admitted to practice each year.

The Legal Training and Research Institute has a two-year curriculum.
Figure 2.1 indicates that the Institute curriculum heavily stresses

FIGURE 2.1
Functions of the Legal Training and Research Institute

1. Major Functions
   (1) Training for Legal Apprentices
   (2) Continuing Legal Education for Judges

2. Training for Legal Apprentices

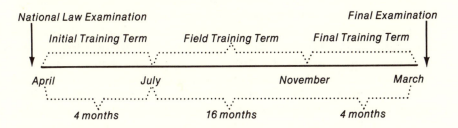

3. Continuing Legal Education for Judges
   (1) Training of Assistant Judges and Judges of Summary Courts
   (2) Judicial Research

practical instruction. Two-thirds of the time spent there is devoted to "field training," a term given to the four four-month periods spent by the students as clerks in the field to practicing attorneys, procurators (i.e., prosecutors), and civil and criminal judges. In addition, the teaching by the faculty of the Institute is geared to practical instruction; the faculty is composed of practicing attorneys, judges, and procurators temporarily appointed by the Supreme Court. Through this curriculum students can quickly assimilate the practical skills needed in day-to-day professional activities after graduation.

Based on the example of the civil law system of continental Europe, Institute graduates immediately become judges, procurators, or attorneys. Of the 500 graduates of the Legal Training and Research Institute each year, usually about 70 to 80 become judges, 40 to 50 procurators, and the rest attorneys.[24] For those accustomed to the yearly entrance in the United States of thousands of law school graduates into the ranks of attorneys, it is staggering to consider that in Japan only about 370 do so at the same time.

The comparatively small number of attorneys in Japan and the relatively high fees they charge prevent most Japanese from consulting an attorney if they have a dispute with someone.[25] In this way, the Japanese system has been able to maintain the key Tokugawa/Confucian value of non-litigiousness. As a result, the traditional Japanese norm persists of resolving problems without resorting to litigation. In 1979, for example, 387,000 law suits were filed in Japan. In West Germany, meanwhile, in 1974 there were about 2,000,000 and in England in 1979, 1,990,000, as shown in Table 2.1. If we then compare the population figures of these countries, the frequency of litigation in West Germany and England is nine times greater than in Japan. This figure does not by any means suggest that the Japanese have fewer disputes and arguments than do the Germans and English. What it does show is that the Japanese are still far less prone to use the courts to settle their quarrels.[26] Furthermore, by spending a relatively small amount of money, time, or energy on litigation compared to the West, the Japanese system can devote more resources to benefit society in more tangible ways, i.e., by the production of goods.

It is equally misleading to compare without explanation the raw numbers of attorneys practicing in Japan and the United States. Although it is true that the United States has per capita twenty-five times as many attorneys as Japan, the Japanese have many people who perform tasks that we associate with attorneys in the United States. Although not attorneys per se (since they are not graduates of the Legal Training and Research Institute and are not admitted to practice law), they are quasi-lawyers.[27] One type of quasi-lawyer in Japan is the judicial scrivener, who is empowered to draft court documents, transfer title to land, and give legal advice in these matters. Another type of quasi-lawyer found in Japan is the administrative scrivener; those in this group draft the legal documents which individuals submit to government offices. Two more groups of quasi-lawyers in Japan are the "benrishi" and the "zeirishi." Benrishi can give legal advice on patent and trademark matters and even represent clients in court. Zeirishi can give legal advice in tax matters and represent their clients before the Tax Office in Japan. Attorneys and public accountants are ipso facto qualified as zeirishi. Others, to be accredited as zeirishi or benrishi, must pass an exam.

One more class of quasi-lawyers in Japan is comprised of graduates of universities who specialize in law at the university level and then work in corporate or governmental legal departments. In the Japanese university system, unlike that of most American universities and colleges, students can "specialize" in law. Undergraduate courses in law are taught by professors of law. Virtually all of these professors did not graduate from the Legal Training and Research Institute and are not empowered to practice law.

Since majoring in law at the university level is so common in Japan, many Japanese will tell Americans when they first meet that they specialized in law. The American should not take this statement to mean that his new acquaintance is a lawyer. The only way one can become an attorney in Japan is by graduation from the Legal Training and Research Institute. However, these Japanese are correct when they say they specialized in law; the expression, though, has a different meaning in the two countries. To specialize in law in Japan is similar to majoring in law, assuming there were such a major, at an American university.

One who majors in law at a Japanese university does not by any means have the type of legal knowledge that lawyers in the United States or Japan possess. Instead, the individual has been instructed, mainly through the lecture method, in the general content and interpretation of the more important code provisions of Japan.[28] Individual fact situations and cases are not discussed; systemic development of theory is common.

Since so few applicants are admitted each year to the Legal Training and Research Institute, most of the graduates of Japanese universities who specialize in law go to work for corporations or governmental agencies.[29] Most Japanese corporations, especially the major ones, have corporate law departments.[30] Unlike the United States, most corporate law departments rarely have any lawyers employed there; instead, the members of the corporate law departments are, for the most part, university graduates who specialized in law.[31]

The American negotiating a contract with a Japanese company must,

Table 2.1
Civil Litigation Cases of First Instance

Japan (1979)		
Summary Court:	134,243	
Ordinary civil		67,910
Bill/check		2,494
Civil mediation applied		58,336
Provisional seizure/disposition		5,503
District Court:	166,113	
Ordinary civil		93,732
Promissory note/check		21,364
Administrative		761
Civil mediation applied		776
Insolvency		2,783
Provisional seizure/disposition		46,697
Family Court:	85,955	
Adjudication (B)		5,396
Mediation		80,559
High Court:	252	
Administrative		252
Total	386,563	

Great Britain (1979)		
County Court:	1,659,064	
High Court:	330,603	
Chancery Division		13,848
Queen's Bench		149,244
Family Division		167,511

West German (1974)		
Summary Court:	929,061	
Include		
Ordinary civil		
Documents, Bills, Checks		
Interdiction*		
Public summons*		
District Court:	541,571	
Include		
Ordinary civil		
Documents, Bills, Checks		
Provisionary seizure/disposition		
Matrimony, Childhood, Interdiction		
Other Courts:	531,032	
Labour Court		297,162
Finance Court		21,963
Social Court		154,218
Administrative Court		57,689
Total	2,001,664	

*Interdiction and Public summons amounts, not given separately,
total approximately 18,000 (1967)

Sources: Japan: *Shihō tōkei nenpō* (for 1979)
Great Britain: *Judicial Statistics,* 1979
West Germany: *Anweltsblatt,* 1976, pp. 81, 328–29

Taken from Kahei, "The Law Consciousness of the Japanese,"
The Japan Foundation Newsletter 5, 10 (February/March 1982).

therefore, keep in mind that in the usual case he will not be dealing with an attorney. Instead, he will be dealing with the members of the company's legal department. It is important for the American to determine how much experience his Japanese counterpart has. Clearly, he will not have the legal education background that an American attorney will have.[32] If he has been in the corporate law department for some time, however, he will have an immense amount of experience to draw upon. Although his legal education background is obviously less than that of an American attorney, he will develop in the course of his work as an employee of the corporate law department practical legal skills tailored to the particular needs of his company.

In most cases, the services of an attorney in Japan are not sought until the party decides he has no viable alternative except litigation. Japanese corporations rarely use attorneys for their normal work. The American negotiating a contract in Japan will be struck by the absence of attorneys representing the Japanese company in the drafting stage. A lawyer, if involved at all by the company, will usually act behind the scenes as an "advising attorney" to double-check the contract after it has already been drafted. Unlike in the United States, companies seldom involve attorneys in their decision-making process. The Japanese business law system in this regard is somewhat akin to that of England. The members of the corporate law departments of Japan are comparable to the solicitors of England in that both handle day-to-day contract negotiation and drafting matters. Japan's attorneys, on the other hand, play a similar role to that of the barristers of England in that the work of both usually relates to litigation.

Thus, the role of attorneys in the contract negotiation process in Japan differs greatly from their role in the United States. In the United States, attorneys play an integral role in the process. Clients rely not only on the attorneys' skills as contract drafters but also on their advice about negotiations and on their business judgments. Much of the work of the American business lawyer involves the creative solving of a client's problems. In contrast, in Japan the business client usually consults an attorney only after having completed negotiation of the contract. The attorney rarely participates in the initial business negotiations, often the most crucial part of the contract negotiation process, but simply rewrites the contract language and ties up the loose ends. Some Japanese attorneys have told the author that even their power to redraft the contract language may be limited if it has already been approved by the department's section chief, the "kacho" (a person of substantial responsibility and importance in the company). Frequently, the business client may ask the Japanese lawyer to examine not the entire contract draft, but only a small part—as small as one paragraph!

To sum up, attorneys in the United States and Japan play far different roles. In the United States, attorneys not only handle lawsuits but frequently use their verbal and analytical training to give counsel on business negotiations and decisions. As we have seen, though, Japanese attorneys do not receive this type of training; theirs is far more oriented to practical litigation skills and the drafting of contracts. This training, naturally enough, reflects their type of practice. In a recent survey, for example, attorneys in Tokyo stated that litigation matters comprise 72 percent of their work; attorneys in the countryside estimated the amount as 84 percent.[33] Not surprisingly, since so much of their work centers around litigation, most attorneys in Japan have their offices in large cities with district courts. Tokyo and Osaka are the cities with by far the most attorneys' offices.[34]

The Japanese judicial system resembles the general state court system in the United States. There are trial courts, an intermediate court of appeals, and a supreme court. Japan is divided into forty-nine judicial districts, with the usual court in Japan of original jurisdiction being the District Court. Most District Court cases are heard by a single judge (there are no juries in Japan today).[35] The largest court, and the most important, is the Tokyo District Court. Although the District Court is the usual court of original jurisdiction, the Summary Courts handle lesser civil and criminal matters. Currently, the jurisdiction of the Summary Courts in civil matters is limited to ¥900,000 (about $3,800).[36] In addition, the Family Courts have plenary jurisdiction for family and juvenile matters.

Civil court appeals from the Summary Court go to the District Court, while criminal appeals go directly from the Summary Court to the High Court (the general court of appeal in Japan).[37] District Court appeals and appeals from quasi-judicial governmental bodies go to one of the eight High Courts of Japan. The High Courts are located in different areas of the country. Just as the Tokyo District Court is the most important of the forty-nine District Courts of Japan, so the Tokyo High Court is the most important of the High Courts. Although normally a court of appeal, in one significant situation the High Court sits as a court of original jurisdiction. Pursuant to the law creating the Japan Fair Trade Commission (or JFTC, as it is often referred to), cases filed by the JFTC are adjudicated by the High Court of Tokyo sitting as a court of original jurisdiction.[38] Each case before the High Court is heard by a panel of three judges.

Japanese law provides in commercial cases for two opportunities to appeal a decision of a lower court. The first appeal is called kōso" and the second "jōkoku." The party who loses at trial can file a kōso appeal for an alleged error in fact-finding as well as an alleged error in law.[39] In civil cases, the grounds for jōkoku appeal are two: (1) an error in the interpretation of the Japanese Constitution and (2) an error in law which clearly affects the litigation's outcome.[40] Figure 2.2 illustrates the court system.

The Supreme Court of Japan, which sits in Tokyo, is composed of fifteen justices. The Court conducts hearings and renders decisions as either a petty bench court or a grand (i.e., full) bench. The petty benches are three in number; each consists of five justices. The grand bench must sit to hear

(1) cases in which a determination is made of the constitutionality of a law, ordinance, regulation, or disposition as a result of a litigant's contention (excluding those cases in which the opinion is the same as that of a previous grand bench decision holding such a law, ordinance, regulation, or disposition to be constitutional);
(2) cases other than those previously mentioned in the preceding item when the law, ordinance, regulation, or disposition in question is held to be unconstitutional;
(3) cases in which an opinion regarding the interpretation and application of the Constitution or of any other law or ordinance is contrary to that of a previous Supreme Court decision.[41]

In regard to Supreme Court appointments, only ten of the fifteen justices must be attorneys, procurators, judges, or law professors. The sole requirements for the remaining five are that they have "broad vision and legal knowledge" and be not less than forty years old.[42] The rationale for placing non-legally trained people on the Supreme Court is that they broaden the collective outlook of the Court, an especially important consideration in light of the significant policy issues they must decide.[43] Inevitably, however, the so-called 5-5-5 rule has been followed as to Supreme Court appointments. This unwritten quota rule provides for five of the justices to be chosen from the judiciary, five from the ranks of procurators and law professors, and five from among practicing attorneys.[44] The Chief Justice of the Japanese Supreme Court is appointed by the Emperor based upon the Cabinet's designations;[45] the other justices are appointed by the Cabinet.[46]

The background of judges is one of the most significant differences in the legal systems of the United States and Japan. In the United States judges usually take office by appointment, often after distinguished careers as attorneys. In Japan, where the civil law system governs, judges begin careers on the bench after graduation from the Legal Training and Research Institute (often at the age of twenty-six or twenty-seven). The first years of a judge's career in Japan are usually spent as an assistant judge being rotated regularly to various courts. After ten years, the person then becomes a full judge.

FIGURE 2.2
The Japanese Court System

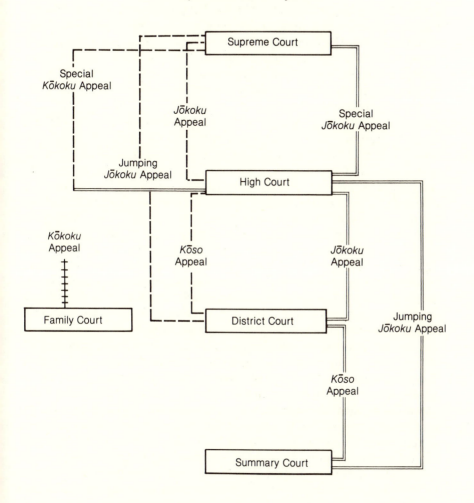

═══	When the Summary Court is the court of first instance
─ ─ ─	When the District Court is the court of first instance
++++	When the Family Court is the court of first instance

Neither Japanese attorneys nor judges enjoy the prestige that accrues to their counterparts in the United States. One reason may again relate to the traditional Japanese aversion to litigation; perhaps this dislike has spilled over to those involved in the process. Another reason may stem from the greater public awareness of American attorneys and judges. Due to the greater frequency of litigation in the United States, the newspapers report more cases and give resulting publicity to those involved. Since the Japanese are more loath to engage in litigation, fewer disputes reach the courts and thus the public eye. Also, judges in Japan rarely if ever issue the sweeping types of decisions like those of American courts which receive great media coverage and can ultimately transform society. It may well be, however, that this difference in prestige stems from the very natures of the two judicial systems. Acting under the civil law traditions of Japan, the judge will simply call the attention of the public to the specific statute which he is invoking as authority. In contrast, under the common law system the judge enjoys more free-wheeling powers. Japanese judges rarely if ever write philosophical decisions which the populace may discuss at length. American judges, on the other hand, frequently write such opinions, for example in dissent and with the hope of thereby changing the future votes of other judges. Often an American judge will issue an opinion changing the law because he sees the court as the vehicle to do so; rarely, if ever, will a Japanese judge so view the court. In fact, an analysis of Japanese opinions leads one to believe that many Japanese judges see their roles as guardians of the values of Japan that have guided that country for hundreds of years.[47]

As American lawyers deal increasingly not only with businesses and attorneys from Japan coming to the United States but also with clients doing business in Japan, they have developed a rising interest in establishing offices in Japan. In recent years, American attorneys have literally besieged the Japanese government with requests to open up branches of law offices in Japan.[48] For the most part, the Japanese have adamantly refused to change their restrictive policies on visas for American attorneys. In addition, stringent Japanese bar association rules stand as another impediment in the quest of American attorneys to open offices in Japan. The Americans argue that the Japanese resistance to the practice of law in Japan by Americans in the face of the ability of the Japanese to do so in the United States (*arguendo* they have passed the bar examination in that jurisdiction) has reached the status of a formal trade barrier.[49]

In 1977 the New York City law firm of Milbank, Tweed, Hadley & McCoy did open its own office in Tokyo to advise such American clients there as the Chase Manhattan Bank on United States law.[50] Many

Japanese attorneys filed protests against the opening of the office, pointing out that no member of the firm was admitted to practice in Japan. The firm countered by stating that its members were not advising on Japanese law but rather on foreign (i.e., United States) law. The firm argued that the attorney-enabling statute in Japan does not prohibit people not permitted to practice law in Japan from giving advice on foreign law.[51] This interpretation is not supported by any statute or court holding but is buttressed by the fact that Japanese attorneys receive no training in, nor are they ever examined on, foreign law.[52] At any rate, despite the protests, the Milbank firm still operates in Japan today. Milbank apparently has acceded in some degree, however, to the Japanese protests since its office door first lists the names of the resident partners in Tokyo and then below them the firm name. In addition, the firm reportedly consented to limit its practice in Japan to a few of its major American clients doing business there.[53]

Other major United States firms, such as Baker & McKenzie and Coudert Brothers, now have offices in Tokyo through affiliated Tokyo law firms. Most of the clients in their Tokyo offices are Japanese.[54] In the usual case, however, the Japanese have used the visa weapon to frustrate the efforts of American attorneys to operate there.[55] At the time this book went to press, American attorneys hoped that the barriers to their opening offices in Japan could be resolved within the context of the trade liberalization talks being held between officials of the United States and Japanese governments.

Despite these restrictive policies, some Americans currently practice law in Japan. Many of them came to Japan after World War II to handle the legal matters of SCAP (Supreme Commander for the Allied Powers) and to assist in the international military affairs trials. The others came to handle non-occupation related legal matters. In 1949, the Supreme Court of Japan enacted regulations allowing them to practice law in Japan.[56] In 1955, an amendment to the Japanese statute governing the practice of law repealed this regulation, but those foreigners already practicing law in Japan were covered by a "grandfather clause" that allowed them to continue practicing as long as they lived in Japan.[57] Those Americans still practicing law in Japan under that clause are the remnants of this group.

An increasing number of American attorneys, many directly out of law school, go to Japan each year to work for Japanese law firms as "trainees" or "advisors" for a period of usually two years. Although they cannot practice law in Japan on their own, the Americans can work under the supervision of a Japanese lawyer. Many of the Americans, though, find this experience surprisingly frustrating. Since their work consists for the most part of drafting documents in English and assisting in international trade matters, those who wish to learn all they can about domestic Japanese law may find it difficult to do so. Those with competence in Japanese find frustrating the realization that their position cannot become a permanent one.

NOTES

1. The Japanese group their periods of history since 1868 by the name of the ruling emperor. Thus, the title Meiji Era denotes the period of history when the Emperor Meiji was the ruler of Japan. The current period in Japan is the Showa Era.

2. The importation of Chinese ideas by the Japanese legal system has been described by one commentator as a "great watershed in the development of Japanese law." B.J. George, Jr., "The Right of Silence in Japanese Law," in *The Constitution of Japan, Its First Twenty Years, 1947-67* 257 (D. Henderson ed. 1968).

3. *See, e.g.*, Stevens, "Japanese Law and the Japanese Legal System: Perspectives for the American Business Lawyer," 27 *The Business Lawyer* 1259 (July 1972).

4. There were people, though, who became experienced in the ways of the courts and who did counsel litigants. These were the inn-keepers of Tokyo (then called Edo) who listened to the tales of the litigants who had journeyed to Edo to have their cases heard and gradually developed an expertise in this area. *See, e.g.*, Robert Brown, "A Lawyer by Any Other Name: Legal Advisors in Japan," in *Legal Aspects of Doing Business in Japan 1983* 201, 223 (Lincoln and Rosenthal chmn. 1983) [hereinafter Brown].

5. The years of 1603 to 1868 are known in Japanese history as the Tokugawa era. In 1603 Tokugawa Ieyasu unified rule in Japan and as the shogun exercised political domination. This era continued under his family's rule until the Meiji Restoration in 1868.

6. Professor Dan Fenno Henderson has dramatically shown how this societal pressure not to take one's disputes to court worked in a typical case. 1 D. Henderson, *Conciliation and Japanese Law: Tokugawa and Modern* 127-170 (1965).

7. Noda, "Nihon-Jin no Seikaku to Sono Ho-kannen" ("The Character of the Japanese People and Their Conception of Law"), 140 *Misuzu* 2, 14-26 (1971), translated and quoted in *The Japanese Legal System* 305 (H. Tanaka ed. 1976) [hereinafter cited as Tanaka]. Thus, when Rinsho Mitsukuri was commissioned to translate the French Civil Code into Japanese for possible adoption in Japan, he was stumped as to how the French expression droits civil could be translated into Japanese. Mitsukuri described the situation in this way: "Whereupon at that time I translated the words *droits civil* as minken [people's powers or authority] there was an argument over what did I mean by saying that the people have power [ken]. Even though I tried to justify it as hard as I could, there was an extremely furious argument.... " Mukai and Toshitani, "The Progress and Problems of Compiling the Civil Code in the Early Meiji Era," *Law in Japan: An Annual* 25, 30-33 (1967). Mitsukuri's recitation of this

episode indicates how difficult it was for many Japanese to accept the concept of people having "rights." "Kenri," the word that Mitsukuri eventually decided to use as the Japanese equivalent of droits civil has kept the meaning given it by Mitsukuri. Tanaka, *supra*, at 305.

8. One professor has observed that in Japan "not only are there many instances where written agreements are not drafted, but even when written agreements are drafted their contents are generally very simple and in many cases include only the most important elements." Kawashima, "The Legal Consciousness of Contract in Japan," 7 *Law in Japan: An Annual* 1, 15-16 (1974). The Chinese share the traditional antipathy of the Japanese toward lengthy contracts. One American lawyer has commented that "the Chinese are always asking why we want so much detail.... They say, 'Can't we just shake hands? If we have a problem, we'll work it out.' Rob Ross, "S.F. Firms Make Presence Felt in Chinese Capital," *Los Angeles Daily Journal*, November 3, 1981, at 1, col. 2.

9. Professor Haley of the University of Washington School of Law has written that in Japan one's reputation for trustworthiness is such an integral feature of the business landscape that it "can become a necessity of life." Haley, "Sheathing the Sword of Justice in Japan: An Essay on Law Without Sanctions," 8 *Journal of Japanese Studies* 265, 279 (Summer 1982).

10. Some observers have commented that it is not just the Japanese but Eastasians in general who strongly tend to emphasize compromise rather than confrontation in all their relationships. *See, e.g.,* R. Hofheinz and K. Calder, *The Eastasia Edge* 112 (1982).

11. W. Lockwood, *The Economic Development of Japan* 5-7 (1968).

12. H. Borton, *Japan's Modern Century* 42, 53-54 (rev. ed. 1970).

13. It was Bismarck himself who especially urged the Japanese to adopt the German system as a model. He argued that the German system with its strong monarchy and control by the elite was the best prototype for Japan. It is interesting to note that one reason why the common law system of the United States and England was ultimately rejected by the Japanese as a model is that it requires its judges to have a great analytical ability; Japan had few such trained people at the time. *Cf.* Henderson, "Some Aspects of Tokugawa Law," 27 *Wash. L. Rev.* 85, 91 (1952).

14. Adam Meyerson, "Why Are There So Few Lawyers in Japan," *Wall Street Journal*, February 9, 1981, at 16.

15. Geoffrey Murray, "Advice to the Lovelorn—Japanese Style," *Los Angeles Times*, October 8, 1982, Sec. V, at 27.

16. If one has taught law for five years in Japan, this rule can be waived. Bengoshi Ho [Lawyers' Law], Art. 5 (3) (Law No. 205, June 10, 1949).

17.   The salary is approximately the same as that received by newly appointed public officials who are university graduates. Rules Concerning Legal Apprentices, Arts. 2-3 (Supreme Court Rule No. 15, 1948).

18. Japan is a country where each stage of one's life is seemingly governed by the examination system; many Japanese argue that the examination to enter the Legal Training and Research Institute is the most difficult in the nation. The passing rate from 1949 to 1975 is detailed as follows:

Year	Number of Applicants	Those who Passed the Mutiple-Choice Type Test	Those who Passed the Final Exam	Percentage of Success
1949	2,514	—	265	10.5
50	2,755	—	269	9.8
51	3,648	—	272	7.5
52	4,765	—	253	5.3
53	5,141	—	224	4.4
54	5,172	—	250	4.8
55	6,306	—	264	4.2
56	6,714	—	297	4.4
57	6,920	—	286	4.1
58	7,074	—	346	4.9
59	7,819	—	319	4.1
60	8,302	—	345	4.2
61	10,921	2,092	380	3.5
62	10,802	1,931	459	4.2
63	11,725	2,030	456	3.9
64	12,728	2,017	508	4.0
65	13,681	2,258	528	3.9
66	14,867	2,225	554	3.7
67	16,460	2,244	537	3.3
68	17,727	2,322	525	3.0
69	18,453	2,326	501	2.7
70	20,160	2,157	507	2.5
71	22,336	2,821	533	2.4
72	23,425	2,407	537	2.3
73	25,259	2,484	537	2.1
74	26,708	2,419	491	1.8
75	27,791	2,343	472	1.7

Tanaka, *supra* note 7, at 577.

19. There are in Japan a substantial number of individuals who spend many years studying for the entrance examination to the Legal Training and Research Institute before they pass it; many others spend many years studying for it, taking the exam each time, but never do pass. In understated humor typical of the Japanese, these people are called "ronin," the Japanese word for the samurai of the Tokugawa era who because they did not have a master to serve roamed Japan searching for one. Some observers of the Japanese scene have argued that these people represent today a very inefficient use of labor. *See, e.g.*, Haruo Abe, "Education of the Legal Profession in Japan," in *Law in Japan—The Legal Order in a Changing Society* 153, 162 n.17 (A. von Mehren ed. 1963).

20. Brown, *supra* note 4, at 227.

21. The Legal Training and Research Institute is directly under the supervision of the Japanese Supreme Court.

22. *See. e.g.*, Brown, *supra* note 4, at 448.

23. There is a test given before one can graduate from the Legal Training and Research Institute; failure, however, is rare. Those who do fail can take the final examination again after one more year of instruction at the Institute.

24. Discussion with Shigeo Kifuji, Counselor at the Japanese Ministry of Justice, on June 29, 1982.

25. One publication recently described Japanese attorneys' fees as follows:

Those law firms in Japan which are dubbed or self-acclaimed as international offices generally charge for their services (litigation or otherwise) on a time charge basis. The rate, whether quoted in dollars or yen, is roughly in the range of $50.00 to $200.00 per hour. The $50.00 figure clearly ought to be considered on the low side and would perhaps be applicable to the work of a new associate....

For non-contentious matters, e.g., contract drafting, opinion letter, services are generally charged on a lump sum basis. The actual amount is in fact determined by the attorney after the service has been substantially completed. The amount is rather roughly calculated on the basis of the time spent for the service and the value of the service to the client.

Contentious matters, normally requiring negotiations and/or litigation, are generally hand-led by both plaintiff and defense attorneys on the basis of an initial non-returnable lump sum fee calculated as a percentage of the amount claimed or in dispute, and a success fee. The success fee for the plaintiff attorney would be earned only if there is success and would be calculated as a percentage of what the plaintiff received in judgment or settlement. The success fee for the defense attorney would be calculated on the amount the claim was reduced, whether in judgment or settlement. In all cases, court costs and out-of-pocket expenses are to be for the client's account.

The actual calculation of fees is guided by the fee rules of the Japan Federation of Bar Associations. The guidelines are just that—guidelines. They are not mandatory, but it is said that they are for the public benefit, in that the clients will have an idea whether the fee is excessive or not.

The guidelines provide a sliding percentage scale depending upon the yen amount. For example, 15% of the first ¥500,000, 12% of the next ¥500,000, and 10% of the next ¥2 million. Since the initial fee is based on the amount claimed, it is easy for the attorney to set the initial fee with the client. However, because the success fee is based on the "amount" of success, one could not say beforehand what percentage would apply.

Attorneys often solve the problem by proposing the success fee percentage indicated in the guidelines which corresponds with the attorney's estimate of the actual outcome.

The fee guidelines indicate that the initial fee and success fee may each be set within a range of 30% below and 30% above the amount calculated in accordance with the guidelines, all depending upon the complexity and difficulty of the case.

Shown [here] are the sample initial fee percentages, for both plaintiff and the defense attorneys, resulting from guideline calculations and the suggested range. The success fee percentage would be the same as that for the initial fee, assuming either full recovery by the plaintiff or complete victory to defendant.

[For comparisons, compute approximately 235 yen to the US dollar.]

Amount Claimed	Initial Fee
¥10 million	8.45%
	¥591,500-¥1,098,500
¥20 million	6.7%
	¥941,500-¥1,748,500

¥50 million	3.7%
	¥1,291,500-¥2,398,500
¥100 million	4.8%
	¥3,391,500-¥6,298,500
¥500 million	3.4%
	¥11,791,500-¥21,893,500

The guidelines do not distinguish between negotiations and litigation fees, but attorneys generally make a lower fee quotation for negotiations.

It appears that Japanese attorneys often decide that the fee provided by the guidelines is, from the practical point of view, simply too high to propose to the client. Also as one might expect, there is a tendency for the plaintiff attorney to quote on the low side for the initial fee but on the high side for the success fee. The tendency for the defense attorney is generally the opposite. Specific fee proposals are, of course, negotiable. However, Japanese attorneys are not accustomed to negotiating regarding their fee proposals, and, in fact, many old-timers are very, very reluctant to negotiate at all with individuals and corporate clients alike.

"Japanese Fee Practice," *International Lawyers' Newsletter* 1 (July/August 1981).

Note: The Japanese Bar Association has recently revised its compensation standards. The fees for consultation have been raised from ¥5,000 for one hour to ¥5,000 for thirty minutes. Work outside the office has been raised from ¥10,000 or more per day to ¥20,000 or more. This increase is the first such increase in nine years. This information is taken from the *Japan Newsletter*, edited by Rod Seeman, March 1984, p. 36.

26. Professor Haley of the University of Washington School of Law has argued that the Japanese are not especially reluctant litigators. Rather, he asserts, there is present in Japan the distaste for litigation and the preference for informal dispute resolutions that is found in most societies. What the Japanese have done is simply to use institutional arrangements to protect this preference from societal erosion. Haley, "The Myth of the Reluctant Litigant," 4 *Journal of Japanese Studies* 359 (Summer 1978).

27. In the early 1970s, registered quasi-lawyers in Japan totalled about 65,000 — excluding the law graduate category on which figures are not maintained. *See* Bolz, "Judicial Review in Japan," 4 *Hastings Int'l and Comp. L. Rev.* 87, 121 n.144 (1980).

28. Since Japan's legal system is a progeny of the civil law system, the study of law in Japan is centered around the six most important codes of Japan (called in Japanese, "the Roppo"), the Constitution, Codes of Civil and Criminal Procedure, Civil, Penal, and Commercial Codes.

29. Only 0.3 percent of all law department graduates will ever pass the exam to enter the Legal Training and Research Institute. Brown, *supra* note 4, at 237.

30. These corporate law departments are a relatively new phenomenon in Japan, since most were formed in the 1970s. *See* "Concerning the Roles of the Legal Departments of Typical Japanese Enterprises," *Commercial Law Center, Inc.* 1 (1979).

31. As of June 1982 only five attorneys were directly employed by corporations in Japan. The statute regulating the practice of law in Japan states

that attorneys cannot work directly for companies without the permission of their bar association. Bengoshi Ho, Art. 30(3) (Lawyers' Law, Law No. 205, June 10, 1949).

32. Many members of Japanese corporate law departments, though, especially the younger ones, have studied in an LL.M. or M.C.L. program at an American law school.

33. Kahei, "The Law Consciousness of the Japanese," *The Japan Foundation Newsletter* 5, 10 (February/March 1982).

34. Most law offices in Japan are very small by American standards. The largest office in Tokyo, for example, has about twenty-five attorneys while most have one or two.

35. Japan did have at one time provision for juries. The jury system was widely unpopular, and the statute providing for juries has been suspended since 1943. An Act to Suspend the Jury Act (Baishin Ho no Teishi ni Kansuru Horitsu) (1943 c.88). *See* , *e.g.*, K. Saito (Bashin) (Jury) in *Keiji Hogaku Jiten (Dictionary on Criminal Law)*, 62 (Takigawa ed. 1957).

36. Law No. 82, August 24, 1982.

37. Conversation with Judge Junichi Koide of the Tokyo District Court, June 29, 1982.

38. Court Act, Art. 16.

39. Code of Civil Procedure (Minji Sosho Ho) (1890 c. 29), Art. 360.

40. Code of Civil Procedure, Art. 394. Article 395 lists grounds where an error in procedure shall ipso facto be so grave as to be a ground for appeal.

41. Saiban Shoho, Art. 10 (Court Organization Law, Law No. 59, 1947).

42. Ct. Law, Art. 41(1). This statute provides that ten of the fifteen justices must have been either (1) District or High Court judges with at least ten years of experience, or (2) Summary Court judges, prosecutors, lawyers, or law professors with at least twenty years experience.

43. *See. e.g.*, George, "The Japanese Judicial System: Thirty Years of Transition," 12 *Loy. L.A.L. Rev.* 807, 814 (1979).

44. Tanaka, "The Appointment of Supreme Court Justices and the Popular Review of Appointments," 11 *Law in Japan: An Annual* 25, 27-28 (1978). Since 1947 only five justices have been appointed who were not formerly attorneys, judges, procurators, or law professors. Brown, *supra* note 4, at 289.

45. *Const.*, Art. 6(2).

46. *Const.*, Art. 79(1).

47. Hahn, "The Rights of Newspaper Reporters and the Public Welfare Standard in Japan," 11 *Cal. W. Int'l. L.J.* 189, 222 (1981).

48. The Americans argue that Article VIII of the Treaty of Friendship, Commerce, and Navigation between the United States and Japan permits the activities of American lawyers in Japan. *See* Treaty No. 27, 4 U.S.T. 2065 (1953).

49. *See, e.g.,* "U.S. Lawyers Allege Trade Barriers," *The Wall Street Journal,* April 20, 1982, at 35. The Japanese state in response that recent Japanese Supreme Court actions have opened the door for Americans to apply for admission to the Legal Training and Research Institute. Most Americans I have met who are conversant with this issue simply laugh and declare that the Japanese action is of little value. They assert that the nature of the exami-

nation requires a knowledge of the Japanese language beyond that possessed by Americans.

50. Tsuyoshi Fukuda, "Japan," in II *Transnational Legal Practice* 201, 213, 217 (D. Campbell ed. 1982).

51. Bengoshi Ho [Lawyers' Law] (Law No. 205, June 10, 1949).

52. The Japanese counter this argument by insisting that the practice of law is a privilege conferred only by law and requiring an enabling statute.

53. Brown, *supra* note 4, at 458.

54. *Id.*, at 463.

55. One American had her visa application blocked because she refused to promise not to complain about the issue. *See*, Larry Tell, "U.S. Lawyers Want Japan to Open Door to Practice," *The National Law Journal*, May 3, 1982, at 2. Another lawyer told me in June of 1982 that the Japanese had in the past given him a visa but made him promise not to take any depositions while he was in Japan. His story is apparently a common one.

56. Supreme Court Regulation No. 22 of September 1, 1949.

57. Law No. 155 of 1955.

Negotiating with the Japanese   **3**

Negotiating contracts in Japan is akin to a rite because of the unwritten rules that so strongly govern the process. The American businessman or attorney who expects to leap off the plane at Narita Airport and immediately launch into intensive contractual negotiations with the Japanese will be greatly disappointed. Social aspects precede the negotiations—social aspects that cannot be dispensed with, no matter how secondary to the actual negotiations the American may view them. In fact, to view them as secondary is to make a mistake that may well be disastrous for the American in the long run and result in the negotiations being unsuccessful with no contract being executed. Instead, the American should view the social aspects as an integral element of the negotiation process itself; to slight the former is to affect deleteriously, perhaps fatally, the latter.

Even before the American negotiator embarks on his trip to Japan, he must take several steps to procure items that he would not ordinarily use in negotiations with Westerners but that are well-nigh indispensable in doing business with the Japanese. One is the "meishi," the business card (or, as many Japanese call it, the "name card"). If business negotiating is a rite in Japan, then the meishi is a central feature of the rite. Exchanged by businessmen when they meet for the first time, the meishi commonly contains one side in English and the other in Japanese with each side stating the bearer's name, business title, employer, and business address. Figure 3.1 provides an example of a typical meishi. The card serves several functions. Japanese society, for example, is still highly stratified,[1] and the exchange of meishi allows each businessman quickly to be apprised of the other's title, employer, and position in that company.[2] In addition, its use enables the parties to avoid the embarrassments that result when one forgets the other's name.

Figure 3.1
Two Sides of a Typical Meishi

CALIFORNIA WESTERN SCHOOL OF LAW

ELLIOTT J. HAHN
ASSOCIATE PROFESSOR OF LAW

350 CEDAR STREET
SAN DIEGO, CA 92101   (714) 239-0391

准教授　エリオット J・ハーン　法学部　カリフォルニア ウエスタン法科大学

カリフォルニア州 サンデイエゴ市

The American businessman going to Japan not only should take a voluminous supply of meishi with him but also make sure that the meishi is done correctly. Stories in Tokyo abound about Americans carrying incorrect meishi. A Japanese friend once told me of an American sales representative whose Japanese side of his meishi stated that he was a "traveling vagabond."[3] Incorrect meishi to Americans inexperienced in Japanese ways may not seem like a major item, but in the rite of negotiating with the Japanese having correct meishi in one's possession is a must. In addition, there is literally a proper etiquette in Japan for the exchange of meishi. The American should not casually discard the giver's meishi after a quick glance; rather, he should carefully study it for a few seconds and then place it in his wallet, briefcase, or jacket for keeping (I, in fact, keep a file of all the meishi given to me for future reference in case I meet the person again or wish to write or call him). Furthermore, care should be taken to see that the recipient is handed the meishi so that he can read it immediately (i.e., not upside down).

Another item important in business negotiations with the Japanese is gifts. Gift-giving is an important rite in the Japanese business system, and gifts of quality brandy, Scotch, or whiskey to Japanese from Americans at their first meeting are usually greatly prized.[4] Reciprocally, the American can often expect to be given gifts by his Japanese counterparts. The Japanese are very fond of giving gifts (especially during the months of July and December, the gift seasons). Yet the American involved should be cognizant that the customs inherent in this gift-giving are very different from those of the West. When handing someone a gift, for example, the Japanese will often apologize for the gift's lack of grandeur. To a Westerner, this apology after giving a gift may seen odd, to say the least. It may even smack of excessive humility. The Japanese, though, regard the gift as simply a small expression of the good feelings of the giver to the other. By declaring that the gift is only a trifle, the gift-giver does not embarrass the recipient with effusive sentimentality and yet still conveys to the other the depth of his feelings. In this way, the giver allows the recipient to accept the gift comfortably. At the same time, if the recipient of the gift is a Westerner he should be aware of the traditional Japanese aversion to opening the gift in the giver's presence. By not opening the gift at that time, the recipient avoids commenting on the giver's feelings by looking at his gift and thus embarrassing the giver.[5] When the American lawyer or businessman does receive a gift from a Japanese, it is not necessary for him to offer effusive words of gratitude at the time. Instead, they should be saved for the next meeting. The "thank you" should not itself be effusive. The Japanese, for example, simply commonly say, "Senjitsu, domo," "Thanks for the other day."

When the American finally does deplane in Japan with his meishi and gifts, he should not expect business negotiations to be concluded quickly. As we saw earlier, the Japanese view the contractual relationship in a far disparate manner than do Americans. Before they begin the actual negotiation process, the Japanese seek through social activities to discover what the other party is like. To Americans, the word "contract" means a legal agreement defining the rights and responsibilities of the parties.[6] The Japanese, on the other hand, envision a business transaction as an ongoing harmonious relationship between parties committed from the onset to creating a mutually beneficial business and then, once they enter into the relationship, to actively maintaining it as such. Once the contract is executed, the Japanese have traditionally believed that the parties have implicitly agreed that any problem that might arise between them will be resolved in an atmosphere characterized by congeniality and trust. The traditional Japanese contract is, therefore, a strange animal to American lawyers and businessmen. It is a very short (often one page) recital of the parties' rights and obligations in which the parties broadly agree to negotiate any problem that may arise in good faith.[7]

Whereas Americans usually sign contracts simply because the transaction will benefit them, the Japanese go one step further. Traditionally, they are not only looking for profit but also striving to achieve even in a business relationship the spirit of wa (i.e., harmony). It has been written, for example, that the Japanese do not negotiate contracts but rather relationships themselves.[8] The Japanese believe that a contract encompasses a moral as well as a legal obligation. Professor Hattori Shiro, a linguistics professor at Tokyo University, made this point when he wrote that:

Americans carefully observe the law, regulations, and contractual agreements and are a people who make full use of such legal forms. Japanese do not have a sufficiently clear conception of such legal forms and honor and trust in things such as jojo [the surrounding circumstances], giri [moral or social obligations to others and to one's name], ninjo [human feeling], yujo [friendship], and magokoro [sincerity].... It is common knowledge that Americans will observe a contract obligation more closely than Japanese. Conversely it is very clearly stated [in America] that not agreeing does not lead to responsibility toward the other person. When a Japanese agrees with another person, he emphasizes the good will and friendship which gave rise to the agreement rather than the agreement itself. If sincerity also is present, there is not necessarily a hindrance even if the contract itself is not executed as precisely as the words say.... To Americans there is a clear distinction between legal agreements and feelings of friendship. In these circumstances Japanese are preoccupied with a friendly atmosphere and are not careful to see that the agreement itself is thorough.[9]

During initial negotiations the Japanese will often seek to probe the attitudes and ideas of the Westerner on the other side of the bargaining table. The Westerner should not resent this process, although apparently unrelated to the underlying business deal. In attempting to learn the other side's attitudes, personalities, and thinking, the Japanese is seeking to ensure that a long-term business relationship characterized by friendship and trust is also desired by the other company.[10] Thus, this negotiation process may take a longer period of time than if two

American businessmen were involved. Rather than becoming impatient or resenting the delay involved, the American attorney should facilitate this process by being frank about his client's long-term interests and goals. For the discussion to proceed in this way he should take time before the negotiations begin to become as fully informed as possible about not only the overall business picture of his own client but also that of the other side.

A related point to the Japanese desire for the establishment of a long-term harmonious relationship is the Japanese traditional distrust of attorneys.[11] Even today many Japanese oppose the idea of an attorney being involved in the negotiation of a contract. By entering the negotiation process as the representative and advocate of one party, the attorney (they believe) prevents the establishment of the business relationship that they desire. They assume that if the American company involves an attorney in the negotiations the company is dealing in bad faith from the onset. The role of an attorney in contract negotiations, they believe, should be to evaluate the language of the proposed contract after the parties have by themselves hammered out the general parameters of the agreement. If the attorney is instead directly involved in the negotiation stage itself, they believe that he is there because his client is opposed to a resolution in good faith through compromise of any problems that may arise in the negotiation of the contract. The American lawyer should be sensitive to this feeling. From the beginning, he should stress to the Japanese that his role is to help the negotiations flow. Whereas in a typical American contract negotiation session he might often break in and press a position emphatically or reject another flatly, he should take care to see that he displays to the Japanese patience at all times. He should never show any indignation or anger with the Japanese. To lose one's temper is to disrupt the harmonious nature of the relationship that, as we have seen, the Japanese seek to establish and then maintain. Neither the American lawyer nor the businessman should ever flatly reject ideas proffered by the Japanese; such an event would cause the Japanese to lose face.[12] In addition, the American lawyer involved should see that if he represents an American, he himself does not dominate the negotiations to such a degree that his client rarely is heard. To repeat, one of the purposes of the negotiations for the Japanese is to become familiar with the other side.

The lawyer is not the only party involved in the negotiations who should continually remember to be patient; the businessman involved must also keep this point carefully in mind. Patience will be required of them both in many ways. No outward displays of indignation or anger should take place. Wa must be maintained.

The traditionally strong Japanese desire to have an atmosphere of trust and congeniality between the parties leads them to devote much time at the outset to socializing, in an effort to get to know the other side in a personal way. The American should not resent this delay in the business negotiating, time which in the American perception is being spent on "pleasure" rather than "business." The Japanese view of this socializing time is that the time spent on entertainment and socializing has a concomitant relationship to the contract negotiations; it is important that the parties involved in the negotiations also spend time together at dinner or on the golf course so that a relationship of trust and harmony is created that will ultimately serve them well during what they hope will be a long business relationship. The Japanese are seeking by this socializing to establish and then maintain a harmonious relationship between the parties, a relationship that will ensure that once the contract is executed no problems will arise that will not be settled by the parties themselves in an atmosphere of conciliation and harmony.

This socializing time is so important to the business negotiations that the American should not automatically bring his or her spouse to Japan. The negotiator must caution his or her spouse that the spouse will not usually be included in these after-business hours events and that the spouse should not resent this omission. As we have seen, these social events are important in the mind of the Japanese as a vehicle to create an atmosphere of friendship and trust that will benefit the business relationship; thus, invitations to them should be eagerly accepted by the American.[13] In the typical case, the Japanese businessman will invite the visiting foreigner to dinner at one of the myriad of restaurants in Japan (incredible as it may seem, there are more than 70,000 in Tokyo alone) and afterward to a bar or cabaret. Almost as a rule, the Japanese businessman's wife will not accompany her husband, and the American's spouse will not be invited either. This failure to invite the spouse emphasizes how strong a significance the Japanese place on the existence of a strong personal relationship between the parties while they do business together. To the Japanese, the social hours are a necessary carry-over from the business ones and serve to cement the ties that bind the parties together. It is the belief of the Japanese that this cementing is best done by having only the parties themselves participate in the social entertainment.

Negotiating contracts in Japan thus includes all the skills involved in negotiating with Americans—the ability to be articulate, the sense of knowing when to prod the opposition and when to compromise, the ability to keep matters in perspective, and the essential ability of never losing one's manners or patience—as well as many others. To negotiate successfully in Japan, for example, one must in addition possess a strong stomach, liver, and lungs. As we have seen, much time will be spent by the American in Japan with his Japanese counterparts on activities outside of the office, such as dining, that have an essential role in the negotiating process. It is important for the American to realize that during each element of the socializing process the Japanese will be watching him and sizing him up as a business partner. Unless, therefore, he has a strong aversion to any of the parts of the process, he should participate with gusto. In addition, he must not be afraid or embarrassed to stand up in public and have the eyes of a captive audience fastened upon him as he sings popular American songs. Of late, the rage in Japanese business entertainment has been "Karaoke." Karaoke involves going at night to a bar which usually has an incredibly professional sound system with microphones and many cassettes and tapes that contain the music to famous songs but no lyrics. Each visitor, one at a time, will go up to the center of the room and sing the song in front of everyone else while the music is played. Thus the reason why the cassettes and tapes have the music to songs but not the lyrics. No matter how strange or embarrassed he may feel, the American should participate in the goings-on with a smile. A failure to sing in effect "brands" one with a negative stigma to the Japanese who are continually sizing up the person as a potential business partner.[14]

Even the socializing process has rites connected with it. When the American is being entertained by the Japanese at a restaurant or bar, for example, he should not simply pour the liquid refreshment provided (beer, sake, or tea, for example) into his own glass, as the custom in the United States. In Japan, the "civilized" person always pours for his companion and waits for the other person to pour for him. To pour your own drink and to expect the other person to pour his is in effect to make a statement to the group-oriented Japanese that you put your welfare over that of the group.[15]

The social and economic aspects of life in Japan are invariably so intertwined that the social ones will never be absent from the negotiation process. Coffee and other light refreshments, for example, should always be provided by the American at meetings at his office as a way of showing the Japanese that he is as interested in the existence of wa between the parties as they are.[16] In addition the American involved should not at the beginning of any meeting rush into a discussion of the contract provisions. Instead, he should ask the Japanese about their family, hobbies, and background in an effort to demonstrate that he too is seeking to know more about his potential business partner so that friendship and trust can be established. Often, these brief moments of small talk will pay enormous dividends in light of the contractual relationship that ensues.

This socializing process inevitably causes a longer contract negotiation process than that commonly experienced by Americans. The American should not become impatient at the delay. In fact, the American should give no sign that he expects the negotiations to be completed within a stated deadline. The Japanese are notorious for asking Americans when they arrive in Japan how long they intend to be there.[17] The socializing process is then dragged out until the deadline time for the American nears. Knowing that the American's career advancement prospects may hinge on whether he brings home a signed contract, the Japanese are thus able to wheedle from the American significant last-minute concessions that he probably would not have agreed to earlier.[18] To overcome this tactic, I suggest that the American have his airplane ticket be open-ended as to his return flight and that his hotel reservations be done similarly. If asked by his Japanese negotiating opponents how long he intends to stay in Japan, the American should smile and reply "as long as I must" or words to that effect.

Besides the length of the socializing process, there is another reason why an American usually should not expect to achieve a speedily negotiated contract with the Japanese. The typical method of contract approval in Japanese corporations (at least in the larger ones) is significantly different from that in the United States. It is very rare for the Japanese employees of a larger corporation to have authority themselves to agree to contract provisions, as is common in the United States. Instead, the larger Japanese companies usually use a system of group decision making called "ringi-sho."

Ringi-sho is a business practice unique to Japan.[19] In this process a contract is written up by a low-level manager and circulated among all the concerned parts of the Japanese company for their approval. Under the system the draft contract wends its way up the corporate hierarchy, not down. Even though the draft contract goes up the corporate chain of command, it has been wryly written that if a superior does object, the most he can do is put his seal of approval on it upside down.[20] As one can see from Figure 3.2 depicting the typical ringi-sho system in a Japanese corporation, ultimately a consensus on the appropriate course of action is hammered out, although the process does take a considerable amount of time by American standards. The rendering of the ultimate decision on any given significant contractual matter is thus, by American standards, time consuming. What is especially important to Americans involved in contract negotiations with the Japanese is that the inherent need in the ringi-sho process to confer with other individuals in the company and receive their approval invariably makes it exceedingly difficult for a Japanese negotiator to give a definite "yes" or "no" to the foreign businessman with whom he is negotiating. Thus, the American discussing contractual issues with employees of the larger Japanese companies should invariably not expect to receive quick answers to his proposed provisions. What the American should do at the start of the negotiations is to

Figure 3.2.
Japanese Decision-Making Process, "Ringi-sho"

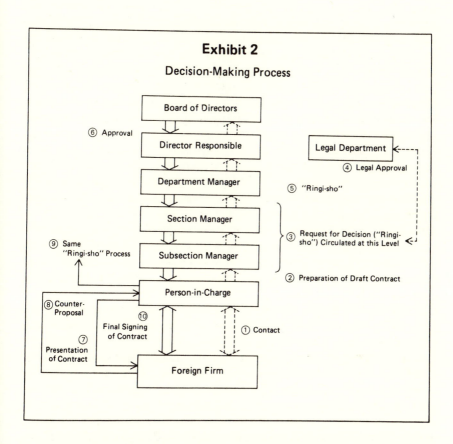

Exhibit 2

Decision-Making Process

Source: Japan External Trade Organization (JETRO), *Contracts and International Trade* 13, "Business Information Service No. 6," reprinted in 1 *The International Contract* 572 (1980).

ascertain the authority of the Japanese on the other side of the bargaining table. Although it is not uncommon in the United States for a negotiator to have authority to bind his employer to a contract by his assent, the opposite is true in Japan. The ringi-sho system is used by the Japanese to reach the consensus which is usually so very important to the Japanese.[21]

One feature of the ringi-sho system especially remarkable to Americans is the lateness of the stage at which Japanese with experience in legal matters enter—and these individuals are frequently not even attorneys. As we have seen, the members of the Japanese corporate law departments are invariably not attorneys. Yet, even these people do not become involved in the contract process until the contract has already been negotiated and received preliminary approval. This feature obviously strongly differs from the practice in the United States where attorneys are involved in the contract negotiation process from the beginning.

A comparison can be made between the roles of U.S. and Japanese attorneys in the contract negotiation process and those of a surgeon and general physician. The U.S. lawyer's role in the American contract negotiation process is similar to that of a physician. He advises his client from the beginning, no matter what the problem. Just as a general physician practices "preventative medicine" to prevent a problem from occurring in the first place, so the American attorney is employed by his client in the contract negotiation process to see that no problems will arise after the contract is executed. The Japanese attorney does not play such a key role. He is a specialist. Just as a surgeon's services are called upon only if a special type of problem arises, so the lawyer in the Japanese contract negotiation process is called upon by his client when a special type of problem occurs. His task is to take the contract as the parties have agreed to it and check the language to insure that it is consistent with their intent. His role, then, compared with his American counterpart's is far less significant and creative in the contract negotiation process.

During the opening and closing of each business meeting, Japanese businessmen may bow formally to the other side's representatives rather than shake their hands. The answer to the question of whether Americans should reciprocate is "sometimes." Those Japanese well versed in Western ways will simply expect the American to shake hands. If the American does decide to bow, a nod of the head or a slight bow is considered acceptable.[22]

Great care should be taken by the American businessman in deciding how the initial contact with the Japanese should be made. This point is especially true for potential exporters of goods to Japan. Japanese companies frequently do not respond to initial correspondence in the way American ones do. They sometimes, for example, do not even answer written inquiries about possible business dealings. The reason is that the Japanese companies usually prefer even from the beginning to discuss these matters in person, not by mail.[23] From the start they desire as much information as possible so that they can decide whether they wish to do business with the exporter. Thus, a more effective method of contact for the American businessman may be to combine contact by letter with personal contact immediately afterward. Failure by the Japanese to respond quickly to an inquiry by letter, though, should not be deemed to indicate a lack of interest on their part. A small Japanese company, for instance, may not be used to being contacted by foreign companies in English. In addition, as we have seen, the decision-making process in Japanese companies, i.e., ringi—sho, is slower and more decentralized than the typical American one; replies may be delayed while the process is used to insure a consensus within the company (see Figure 3.2).

In Japan, personal introductions often play a crucial role in insuring that initial meetings proceed smoothly. If at all possible, the American custom of phoning governmental or business officials directly to set up an appointment should be avoided. Instead, an acquaintance (often a college friend) of the official should arrange an introduction. When he arranges this introduction the go—between will also explain to the Japanese official why the American wishes to see him, what company he represents, and his position in the company.[24] The use of the intermediary is also recommended because if the choice is a good one he will have a strong relationship with the Japanese official; that relationship's aura often will carry over into the American's dealings with the Japanese and lead the latter to be more favorably disposed to the American's ideas.[25]

The strong role of intermediaries in the Japanese business law system is due in part to the emphasis on trustworthiness. The Japanese often will not do business with those they believe they can't trust. One reason for this emphasis is the weakness of the remedies available in Japan against a party in breach of contract. This weakness of legal remedies thus leads the Japanese to avoid doing business with those likely to fail to live up to their contractual obligations.[26] Thus, in many cases unless a Japanese believes you to be trustworthy, either because of your reputation or his own personal knowledge of you from past dealings, he will not do business with you—unless there is an intermediary known to him who will vouch for you. Introductions for an American are therefore essential. One observer has written that "even law firms regularly, if politely, turn away personal clients who do not have proper introductions. Businessmen, government officials, libraries, and schools are often inaccessible without introductions."[27]

Japan is still strongly stratified. For that reason, the American should make sure that his intermediary is of the right social level and, in addition, that the American himself is introduced initially by his intermediary at the proper level of the Japanese company. Pains should be taken so that the American is not introduced at too low a level; otherwise, that low social status will always be associated with him.

Unless fluent in Japanese, the American should conduct his part of the negotiations in English and not in Japanese.[28] Obviously, though, he should take steps to see that the Japanese on the other side understand exactly what he is saying. Although English is a compulsory subject in Japanese schools, most Japanese read and write it far better than they speak the language.[29] Many, in fact, become visibly nervous about speaking English to a native-born speaker. One personal anecdote may illustrate this point. In the summer of 1981 while teaching in Tokyo, I flew to Kochi (a city on Shikoku, the smallest of the four main islands of Japan) to meet with officials of the Asian Legal Research Institute. While there, I was taken to meet a professor who taught English at a local university. After being introduced to him, I asked him, "How long have you been teaching English?" Obviously nervous, he replied after a moment's hesitation, "I am fine, thank you."

If the Japanese person involved is not fluent in English, an interpreter should be used. In the presence of an interpreter, the American should avoid speaking in long paragraphs. Short sentences should be used. If and when a contract is prepared, either the English- or Japanese-language version should be named by both parties as the authoritative one. Furthermore, the document should also clearly state what law is to govern the resolution of any problem that might arise. Legal language should be eschewed as should any type of vocabulary or phrasing used by Americans that might not be precisely translatable from English into Japanese or vice versa.[30] This last point cannot be overemphasized. Legal terms commonly used by Americans should be avoided since even in translation they may have no significance to the Japanese. For example, I was recently asked a question concerning a sale of goods under American law by a Japanese attorney friend. I began to tell him what the applicable law, the Uniform Commercial Code (called the UCC), said. When I mentioned the UCC he looked perplexed. In Japan, the term UCC stands for a type of coffee, and my friend couldn't understand how a particular brand of coffee was relevant to a question about American contract law.

In the contract negotiation, price obviously will be a key item. No matter if it is dollars or yen that is specified as the currency, the rate of exchange should be carefully spelled out. In the last few years, the exchange rate has widely fluctuated from a rate of about 175 ¥ to $1 a few years ago to a rate as of February 1984 of about 235 ¥ to $1. Thus, a Japanese who signed a contract when the exchange rate was less than 200 ¥ to $1 obligating himself to pay $1 for goods is now paying more yen for the same goods. Care should be taken by both parties to see that their contract is specific enough to provide for changes in the exchange rate.

If a Westerner does choose to speak Japanese during the negotiations, he should carefully keep in mind the importance of using the correct level of politeness in addressing the listener. In addressing an old friend or someone who occupies a lower rung on the company or governmental hierarchy, a low level of politeness is used. When one speaks with individuals of the same general social standing who have been met previously, the medium level of politeness is used. In addressing someone who occupies a higher position in the corporate or governmental system, a formal degree of politeness is used. The intricacies and subtleties of these details are so great that the listener is again cautioned to use English unless his Japanese is of the highest proficiency.

As any Japanologist will declare, the Japanese language is a very difficult one to learn. *The Japan Times*, an English-language newspaper published daily in Japan, used to have a column called "Fractured Japanese" written by David Tharp in which stories would be told of Westerners who had mangled the Japanese language. One of these columns ran as follows:

An American investment specialist told me the following story. He was hired as an adviser to a Japanese company due to his expertise in investment portfolios and knowledge of Japanese language.

He had a disastrously hilarious start in his job. He was proud to be the only American in the firm, and everyone remarked on his perfect command of Japanese. Well, almost perfect.

One day some Japanese clients came to the firm's office to discuss investments. Our American linguist met them to make a few welcome remarks before the major business talks started.

The all important introductions were made. The American passed his name card to the clients and said, "Watakushi wa kono kaisha no kōmon desu, dozo yoroshiku." The clients burst into raucous snorts of laughter. Crocodile tears of mirth rolled down their faces.

Our American friend recoiled in horror. He couldn't understand why his fastidiously prepared remarks were subjected to this uproarious reception. He retreated from the room and asked a Japanese colleague to take over while he recomposed his wits.

Shortly, his colleague returned with an explanation of the incident. What the American intended to say was "How do you do, I am an adviser to this company." He thought he was using the word "komon" (adviser). However, he pronounced it "kōmon," the word for anus.

What the Japanese clients heard was "How do you do, I am this company's anus." Following this lesson in practical pronunciation, our friend was much more careful about his long and short vowels.

And while we're on the human anatomy, here's another Fractured Japanese prize winner. An American arrived in Tokyo to study Japanese. At night he would take his texts to a local sakaba (sake house or bar). He assumed (correctly, I think) that one of the best places to get down to the real nitty-gritty with a language is in a drinking establishment.

In one of these forays into the sakaba, the American was asked how he had come to Japan. Our bearded language student decided to answer that he was a vagabond and traveled from one Asian country to another.

He couldn't quite remember what the word for vagabond was but he decided to give it a try anyway: "Ore wa, sorosha desu," he said. The men at the bar lurched across their tables in howls of laughter. The bar hostess spilled bottles of sake as she suppressed a series of guffaws.

The word for vagabond is horosha. The translation of "Ore wa, sorosha desu" is "I am a premature ejaculation." That language slip was good for a few free drinks. Afterward, of course our vagabond was known as soroshasan, Mr. Premature Ejaculation."[31]

If the negotiations are conducted in English without an interpreter being present, the American should keep in mind that when a Japanese constantly answers "yes, yes" to an American's business proposal, it does not necessarily signify that he is, indeed, in agreement. Nor is he trying to mislead the American. Rather, it may be a reflection of the differences between the English and Japanese languages.[32] When Japanese are speaking their own language and using their word for "yes," the word "hai," it does not necessarily mean they agree with the other person's assertions. Instead, "hai" may be used to indicate simply that the listener understands what has been said; its use does not indicate at all whether the listener agrees with the speaker's viewpoint or ideas. Many Japanese will use the English word "yes" in the same way "hai" is used. This linguistic difference between English and Japanese should be remembered by the American.[33] Otherwise, obvious problems may ensue.

The desire of the Japanese to keep the appearance of harmony may also lead them to use "yes" as a device to avoid outright rejection of the point being discussed. To overcome this reluctance of the Japanese, it is often advisable for the American at the beginning of negotiations to indicate that although he too greatly desires to establish and then maintain a harmonious relationship with Japanese, the best way to prevent misunderstandings may be for each party to state frankly their ideas and reactions to the other's ideas with each party taking no offense at the candor. The American should stress that in this way possible future disruptions of harmony may be avoided. Even if the Japanese should quickly agree to this spirit of candor, the American should during the course of the negotiations reiterate how important frankness will be in preventing possible future breaches of the spirit of harmony. Candor, though, is just one of many words and ideas that have a different meaning to Americans than they do to Japanese. The American should therefore keep in mind the thought that true candor will not be an easy item to achieve.

One special bit of advice must be directed to American women who will be involved in contract negotiations with the Japanese. Women have an especially difficult task. The women's liberation movement has had at best a limited influence on Japanese society. The traditional societal idea in Japan that men engage in business and women remain at home and raise the children is still largely true.[34] Not only, therefore, are most Japanese businessmen unused to dealing with women in a business setting, but they also probably wonder why the woman is not home raising children. An American woman involved in business negotiation with the Japanese should be cognizant of this situation from the beginning. Rather than taking offense, she may wish to conceal her true feelings, discuss this difference with the Japanese, and be as businesslike as possible.

Many Japanese men, it should be mentioned, are not inherently chauvinistic; they are simply unaccustomed to having business dealings with women.[35] An American businesswoman I know, for example, came to Tokyo in 1981 to discuss a deal with a Japanese company. She bitterly complained to me in frustration one day that the Japanese subtly refused to discuss business with her. Unaware of the reason, she persuaded me to accompany her to their next meeting to see if I could discern the problem. After the meeting, I told her that the Japanese were confused. They could not understand why the attractive young woman was not in the United States raising a family. The next time we saw the Japanese, she and I both discussed with them the different social values in the United States and Japan; though the Japanese were amazed to hear these details, the problems soon were ironed out.

One aspect of the rite of negotiating contracts with the Japanese that Westerners must also consider is dress. Colorful, non-traditional business clothes should be left in the closet and not brought to Japan. The image that a business executive should portray to the Japanese in the negotiation stage is that of a sober person committed to forging an excellent relationship with the prospective Japanese partner. Care should be taken in dress in order that this image is put in the mind of the Japanese from the start of the negotiating process. If the American is a woman, therefore, she should avoid wearing pants. Conservative dresses and stockings are the rule. Mini-skirts are verboten. For men, traditional three-piece suits and white dress shirts are probably the best clothes to wear in Japan for most of the year. The pervasive heat and humidity in Japan in the summer, though, makes three-piece suits during that time of year an item to be avoided.[36] Light-weight suits and short-sleeve, conservatively colored dress shirts then become the rule.

NOTES

1. *See. e.g.*, R. Benedict, *The Chrysanthemum and the Sword* 43, 47-48 (1946).

2. In the classic work *Japanese Society (1970)*, Chie Nakane wrote that the exchange of meishi "has crucial social implications.... By exchanging

cards, both parties can gauge the relationship between them in terms of relative rank, locating each other within the known order of their society. Only after this is done are they able to speak with assurance, since, before they can do so, they must be sure of the degree of honorific content and politeness they must put into their words" (p. 30).

3. One large airline that has many U.S.-Japan flights advertises that it will supply meishi for its passengers. Reportedly, though, those meishi are rife with errors.

4. Imported liquor is incredibly expensive in Japan, and most Japanese businessmen are very appreciative if they receive as a gift a bottle of, for example, Napoleon brandy (often over $100 a bottle in Japan) or Chivas Regal ($40).

5. *See. e.g.*, "A Word from the Publisher," *The East* 4 (June 1981).

6. *See. e.g.*, *Uniform Commercial Code* Sec. 1-201(11) (1978).

7. *See. e.g.*, Kawashima, "The Legal Consciousness of Contract in Japan," 7 *Law in Japan: An Annual* 1, 15-16 (1974). Professor Kawashima pointed out in the same article that traditionally Japanese contracts have clauses such as: "If in the future a dispute arises between the parties with regard to the rights and duties provided in this contract the parties will confer in good faith (sei-i o motte kyogi suru)," which he called the "confer in good faith" clause, and "will settle the dispute harmoniously by consultation (kyogi ni yori emman ni kaiketsu suru)," the "harmonious settlement" clause. *Id.* at 16. It should be noted that the larger Japanese companies have "learned" from their American counterparts, and today their contracts are usually just as detailed as the typical American ones.

8. *See, e.g.*, Johnson, "The Japanese Milieu and Its Relationship to Business," 13 *Amer. Bus. Law J.* 339 (1976).

9. *Asahi Shimbun*, December 20, 1952, at 6 (morning ed.).

10. Jun Mori, "A Negotiator's Perspective on Negotiations and Communication with Japanese Businessmen," in *Current Leqal Aspects of Doing Business in Japan and East Asia* 47 (J. Haley ed. 1978).

11. The Japanese believe that attorneys destroy wa by stressing their client's position and ignoring a compromise that may better benefit society as a whole. The Japanese are not alone in this belief. An American who is frequently involved in legal negotiations in China has stated that "the Chinese are not quite convinced of the utility of lawyers." *See* Rob Ross, "S.F. Firms Make Presence Felt in Chinese Capital," *Los Angeles Daily Journal*, November 3, 1981, at 1.

12. *See, e.g.*, R. Halloran, *Japan: Images and Realities* 236 (1970).

13. In contrast to the case in the United States, only rarely will the invitation be to the home of the Japanese businessman for dinner. Most Japanese believe that their homes are too small to invite company there (many Japanese refer to their homes as "rabbit hutches").

14. The popularity of Karaoke has even been extended to the Japanese home. Unofficial estimates put the number of home Karaoke units sold in Japan in 1982 at 1.3 million, double the amount sold in 1981. Ronald Rhodes, "What's New in Japanese Consumer Electronics," *The New York Times*, May 8, 1983, Sec. 3 (Business), at 15. Karaoke may even soon be familiar in the United

States. Several Japanese companies have recently announced plans to sell Karaoke sets in the United States. "Karaoke Sets Are Penetrating American Market," *The Japan Economic Journal*, August 2, 1983, at 7.

15. The Chinese, another group-oriented people, have a similar custom. If alcohol is served in China, one doesn't drink by himself. A "civilized" person there instead always lifts his cup in toast to a fellow guest or waits for another diner to toast him. *See. e.g.*, Fox Butterfield, "It's Not All Chinese Banquets," *The New York Times*, February 6, 1983, Section 10 (Travel), at 15.

16. During warm weather, iced coffee is a favorite refreshment of the Japanese. The American should have it available as a choice for his Japanese guests.

17. I have even heard stories about Japanese calling the hotel where the American is staying to determine how long he intends to stay.

18. For a humorous anecdote that makes this point explicit, *see* H. Cohen, *You Can Negotiate Anything* 93-95 (1981).

19. Professor Nakane has stated that what is unique is that in the ringisho process superiors do not force their ideas on juniors. Instead, juniors, based on what they perceive as acceptable, lay their opinions before their superiors and have them adopted. C. Nakane, *supra* at 2, at 65.

20. M. Yoshino, *Japan's Managerial System* 262 (1968).

21. John H. Holdridge, at the time Assistant Secretary of State for East Asian and Pacific Affairs, told the House Subcommittee on Asian and Pacific Affairs of the Committee on Foreign Affairs on March 1, 1982, that decision making in Japan is based on consensus. Many prominent scholars have reiterated this statement. *See, e.g.*, *Far East Law Newsletter* 14, 22 (August 1982).

22. For a humorous explanation of the technique of bowing in Japan, *see* J. Seward, *Japanese in Action* 42, 54-55 (1968). This book, as are all of Seward's works, is a very funny commentary on Japan and the Japanese.

23. This point, it must be emphasized, is not true for all Japanese companies. That most effective Japanese economic institution, the trading company (in Japanese, "sogo shosha"), for example, is well versed in the ways of the West, including that of initial contact by letter. *See, e.g.*, Masayoshi Kanabayashi, "Japan's Big and Evolving Trade Firms: Can the U.S. Use Something Like Them?" *The Wall Street Journal*, December 17, 1980, at 48.

24. To the hierarchy-conscious Japanese, this last point of information is very important. *See, e.g.*, R. Halloran, *supra* note 12, at 236.

25. Apparently the Japanese believe that American intermediaries may be valuable to them in the future. A Japanese student at the Stanford Business School recently was quoted as saying that one reason his Japanese company sent him there was so that he could be in "contact with people who will be America's future managers." Marilyn Chase, "Japanese Still Think There Is Something to Learn in the U.S.," *The Wall Street Journal*, October 20, 1982, at 1.

26. For a discussion of the lack of meaningful sanctions in Japanese commercial law, *see* Haley, "Sheathing the Sword of Justice: An Essay on Law Without Sanctions," 8 *Journal of Japanese Studies*, 265, 266-269 (Summer 1982).

27. *Id.*, at 279.

28. Professor Henderson has written that "foreigners never master written Japanese; they only achieve lesser degrees of ignorance in it." Henderson, "The Role of Lawyers in U.S.-Japanese Business Transactions," 38 *Wash. L. Rev.* 1, 9 (1963). The same point could be made for spoken Japanese.

29. The Japanese educational system emphasizes the ability to read and write English at a sacrifice of the ability to speak the language well. *See, e.g.,* Vivian Salter, "A Gorgeous 'Na' Melody," *The Atlantic* 8 (October 1981).

30. Since Japanese contract law is based on the civil law system, there is no precise equivalent, for example, in the Japanese language of the American legal requirement of "consideration."

31. Tharp, "Fractured Japanese," *The Japan Times*, June 14, 1980, at 2.

32. *See, e.g.,* Henderson, "Japanese Law in English: Reflections on Translation," 6 *Journal of Japanese Studies* 117 (1980).

33. Even many Japanese are often confused about what responses of "yes" and "no" really mean in Japanese. This intrinsic vagueness greatly complicates the task of Japanese poll takers and has spawned the growth of much more complex techniques for poll takers in Japan than the methods used in the United States. *See* Todd Carrel, "Reticence of Japanese Plagues Pollsters," *The Los Angeles Times*, November 11, 1982, Part I-C, at 1.

34. Marriage and childbearing are still the primary consideration, for most Japanese women. It is a paradox in Japan that Japanese women are still largely traditional while the society is so modern. The reason may be the dichotomy in Japan that while the country has reached a high state of scientific and technological development, traditional values are still strong. *See, e.g.,* *Newsletter of the Asiatic Society of Japan* 3 (January 1983).

35. Professor Nakane has written as follows on the subject of discrimination against women in Japan: "Postwar and present-day discrimination against Japanese women is due to the nature of the labor market and the lack of experience of women in newly accessible job areas. Yet these disadvantages are often simplistically viewed as sex discrimination.... It is my view that among the Japanese sex consciousness has never been as strong as among the Americans." J. Trager, *Letters from Sachiko* 187 (1982) (quoting J. Seward, *America and Japan: The Twain Meet* [1981]).

36. During the summer "rainy season" in Japan (roughly May-July), the American's constant companion should be his umbrella—no matter how clear the sky appears.

Doing Business in Japan 4

For the American seeking to do business in Japan, the constant precept to observe is that the Japanese market (indeed, its overall milieu) is a far different one from that of the United States. Strategy, approaches, and tactics that succeed in the United States often will have far different results in Japan.[1] To do business successfully in Japan requires not only a knowledge of Japan but also an approach tailored to the unique economic system that is Japan's.[2]

Many otherwise intelligent Americans have erred in doing business in Japan simply because they did not take the trouble to learn how truly distinctive the Japanese consumer is. One classic story concerns the Betty Crocker cake mix. Since few Japanese homes have ovens, General Mills designed a Betty Crocker cake mix to be prepared in the electric rice cookers so prevalent in the Japanese homes. The product, though, was a total flop. The reason for the failure is that General Mills, unaware of the particular practices of the Japanese, ignored the special regard the Japanese have for rice. Purity of rice is very important to the Japanese, and they thought this purity would be contaminated by cake flavors. One observer in Tokyo compared the General Mills procedure in this case to that of asking an English housewife to make coffee in her teapot.

The story that is the other side of the coin is the incredibly successful one of Mister Donut franchises in Japan. Mister Donut is one of Japan's biggest fast-food businesses and by far its biggest donut operation. With 346 stores as of December 1982, Mister Donut ranks thirteenth among Japan's fast-food companies and third among foreign-begun, fast-food companies.[3] Most observers agree that the major reason for the success of Mister Donut in Japan is that its product and marketing technique has been tailored to Japanese tastes.[4]

Once the American interested in doing business in Japan is cognizant of the particularities of the Japanese market, the threshold issue is how this business should be done. Trade with Japan raises a myriad of questions for would-be exporters, beginning with decisions about the degree of involvement. The approach taken by an American company can run the gamut from the passive designation of a Japanese or American trading company to act as its agent to the creation of a wholly owned Japan-based subsidiary for manufacturing and/or distribution. It may be obvious, but it is essential that the American company obtain expert assistance before these types of decisions are made. For many American companies, though, the question of how to obtain this assistance is often as mysterious as Japan itself. As Japan's economic prowess has grown in recent years, however, so have the sources of expertise. Some major ones are:

(1) government assistance—both the United States and Japanese governments offer some information, albeit limited, on the Japanese business law system as well as market data.

(a) United States government assistance—export help for American companies is offered by the Department of Commerce and its Foreign Commercial Service. On a general level the Commerce Department publishes an international trade magazine called *Business America* that includes information on Japan. On a more specific level the Department of Commerce has issued several publications dealing with Japan.[5]

The Commerce Department also sponsors seminars, trade missions, and commercial fairs. Information on its services is readily available from any of its forty-one district offices. There is even in Washington, D.C., a Japan marketing specialist who can provide specific information and counseling. In Tokyo, the Foreign Commercial Service maintains a permanent display facility (called the U.S. Trade Center) and can help arrange contacts and set up meetings. In addition, quite a few states and even port authorities have offices in Tokyo to promote trade and investment in both countries.[6] These offices supplement the services of the Commerce Department by providing assistance for producers or exporters in their state or port area.

(b) Japanese government assistance—one good source of assistance for Americans interested in business opportunities in Japan is JETRO (the Japanese External Trade Organization), an arm of the Japanese government administered by MITI (the Ministry of International Trade and Industry). Besides its offices in Japan, JETRO has six American offices (New York, Dallas, Houston, Chicago, Los Angeles, and San Francisco) and offers not only background information on a wide range of business matters but even individual advice and assistance. It also has available many pamphlets of much merit on topics of interest to the potential exporter to Japan.

(2) business organizations that specialize in Japan.

(a) American Chamber of Commerce in Japan (ACCJ)—organized by American companies in Japan, this entity publishes periodicals which can be helpful to Americans planning to enter the Japanese market.[7] Its *ACCJ Journal*, published monthly, features analysis of trade issues and case studies of the business experiences of American companies in Japan. For one seeking a business consultant in Japan, the *ACCJ Journal* may be helpful in that many consultants advertise there.[8] The ACCJ also recently published a booklet called *Guidelines to Successful Entry into the Japanese Market*.

It should be noted that the ACCJ does not have a full-time staff and does not provide individual assistance to Americans who wish to enter the Japanese market. It does, however, take an active interest in increasing American exports to Japan; one way it seeks to be of help in this regard is through its publications, many of which are available in Washington, D.C., at the U.S. Chamber of Commerce or the Commerce Department.

(b) Keizai Koho Center—in 1978 the Keidanren (the Japan Federation of Economic Organizations, a prominent group in Japan which represents about 750 major companies and about 100 national associations of business and is the voice of big business there) established the Keizai Koho Center whose purpose is to emphasize both Japan's economic activity abroad and foreign investment in Japan.[9] As is true with the ACCJ, it does not provide individual assistance, but it does publish several periodicals which may be of interest to the potential American exporter. The Keizai Koho Center also annually publishes a booklet called *Japan Periodicals* which lists all the English-language periodicals published in Japan that year.

(3) private consulting services.

(a) trading companies—I will talk about the special role in Japan occupied by trading companies later in this chapter, but for now it should be noted that the larger Japanese and American trading companies can provide market surveys and contacts ranging from potential customers to joint-venture partners. The nine largest Japanese trading companies (Mitsubishi, Mitsui, C. Itoh, Marubeni, Sumitomo, Nissho-Iwai, Kanematsu-Gosho, Tomen, and Nichimen) each have offices in the United States.[10] Besides the large general trading companies, many smaller general trading companies, specialized trading companies, and buying offices for retail stores have offices in the United States. The JETRO publication, *Directory: Affiliates and Offices of Japanese Firms in the U.S.A.* lists their American addresses.

(b) banks—many American banks have offices today in Japan, and quite a few have consulting services available for their customers.

(c) management consulting firms—an increasing number of management consulting services now maintain offices in Japan to help their clients enter the Japanese market. Some of them even help the American company locate Japanese to work for them. In Japan, lifetime employment at a large company is a common desire, and many Japanese consequently shy away from working for a foreign company whose future in Japan may be uncertain. These consulting firms, however, can be of much assistance in this area to a foreign company.

Once the American company does decide to enter the Japanese market, the obvious issue is in what form this entry should take. There are four basic ways by which a product can be exported to the Japanese consumer: (1) trading company; (2) licensing agreement; (3) joint venture; and (4) establishing in Japan a subsidiary. Some American companies have not chosen any of these four routes but rather have chosen simply to establish branch or liaison offices in Japan. Under Japanese law a foreign company doing more than sporadic business in Japan must appoint a representative in Japan, establish a place of business, and register information with the Japanese government regarding the representative and the place of business.[11] No license or other special permission is needed to set up a branch office in Japan (except for regulated businesses such as banks).

The easiest way for an American company to sell its products in Japan is by using a trading company. Former U.S. Senator Adlai Stevenson III recently noted that the "success of trading companies in exporting United States' products has already been demonstrated by foreign trading companies."[12] Prior to 1982, there were trading companies in Japan, Brazil, Korea, and the Southeast Asian nations.[13] In that year, though, the United States enacted a law[14] whose purpose is to "increase exports of U.S. goods and services by encouraging and facilitating the provision of export trade services to U.S. companies through greater use of export trading companies and export trade associations."[15]

Trading companies have an unusually important function in the development of international trade. Their basic role is that of a trade intermediary. Many businesses, especially smaller ones, make products that could compete well in a foreign market, but the individual company may lack the size, skill, and resources necessary to conduct an export trade. The trading companies provide the size, skill, and resources. The new U.S. law allowing U.S. firms, including banks, to set up trading companies is aimed at this very goal—to help small American companies to sell their goods abroad. Under the legislation, an American trading company would arrange financing and shipment of goods, give legal advice, and take care of insurance, documentation, marketing, and promotion.[16]

Of the nations that allow trading companies to exist, those of Japan are by far the most famous.[17] No other country has trading companies as aggressive, extensive, or broad-gauged as Japan's.[18] Japanese trading companies, for example, have of late gone beyond the traditional trading company function of providing trading services to facilitate exports, imports, and related domestic transactions. They have not only become increasingly active as promoters of trade flows but have even made downstream investments and organized groups of companies into ventures which utilized imported raw materials. In recent years they have taken an active role in creating trade flows by developing sources of supply and viable markets.[19]

Today, there are more than 8,000 trading companies in Japan.[20] They handle a large portion of Japan's imports and exports (see Figure 4.1).

FIGURE 4.1

Share of Japan's Trade Handled by Trading Companies

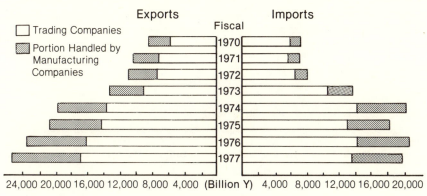

Source: MITI, Trade Business Statistics 1978

In the fiscal year 1977, for example, they handled 65 percent of Japan's exports and 66.9 percent of the country's imports. Of the 8,000 trading companies, by far the most important are the largest sixteen, the sogo shosha, the general trading companies. The Japanese success in exporting goods, it has been said, is primarily traceable to the efforts of the sogo shosha.[21] Four factors make them truly distinctive from the other trading companies: their size, their scope, their information-gathering capabilities, and the diversity of their functions.[22] Each year the sogo shosha handle more than 50 percent of Japan's total foreign trade and account for a major share of domestic transactions.[23] In 1982, for instance, Mitsubishi Corporation, the largest of the sogo shosha, had total sales of more than \$60,000 million, thus making it the biggest company in Japan and the third ranked company in the world in terms of sales. Total annual domestic sales of the nine largest sogo shosha (these nine are Mitsubishi, Mitsui, C. Itoh, Marubeni, Sumitomo, Nissho-Iwai, Kanematsu-Gosho, Tomen, and Nichimen) amounted to ¥ 80.112 trillion (see Table 4.1), a figure almost equal to a third of Japan's g.n.p. (see Figure 4.2).[24]

Table 4.1
Sales of General Trading Companies (Sogo Shosha)

| | | | (Unit: Trillion ¥) |
Company	Annual Turnover	Company	Annual Turnover
Mitsubishi	8.8	Nissho-Iwai	4.2
Mitsui	8.4	Kanematsu-Gosho	2.4
C. Itoh	6.6	Tomen	2.1
Marubeni	6.3	Nichimen	1.8
Sumitomo	5.8		

Note: Sales for the 12-month period ending March 1979.
    Due to the 26% appreciation of the yen in 1978, annual reports of the above companies revealed a decrease in turnover compared with the previous fiscal year.
Source: Company reports

Figure 4.2
Sogo Shosha Sales in 1970, 1975, and 1981

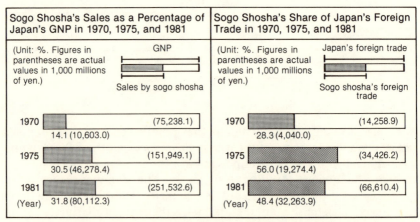

Sogo Shosha's Sales as a Percentage of Japan's GNP in 1970, 1975, and 1981	Sogo Shosha's Share of Japan's Foreign Trade in 1970, 1975, and 1981
(Unit: %. Figures in parentheses are actual values in 1,000 millions of yen.) GNP / Sales by sogo shosha	(Unit: %. Figures in parentheses are actual values in 1,000 millions of yen.) Japan's foreign trade / Sogo shosha's foreign trade
1970 (75,238.1) 14.1 (10,603.0)	1970 (14,258.9) 28.3 (4,040.0)
1975 (151,949.1) 30.5 (46,278.4)	1975 (34,426.2) 56.0 (19,274.4)
1981 (251,532.6) 31.8 (80,112.3)	1981 (66,610.4) 48.4 (32,263.9)
(Year)	(Year)

NOTE: 1970 and 1975 figures are for ten sogo shosha: Mitsubishi Corporation; Mitsui & Co., Ltd.; Marubeni Corporation; C. Itoh & Co., Ltd.; Sumitomo Corporation; Nissho Iwai Corporation; Toyo Menka Kaisha, Ltd.; Kanematsu-Gosho Ltd.; Ataka & Co., Ltd.; and Nichimen Co., Ltd. (now Nichimen Corporation). Omitting Ataka, which was absorbed by C. Itoh & Co. in 1977, 1981 figures are for nine sogo shosha.

Source: Cappiello,"The Changing Role of Japan's General Traders," *Tradepia International* 12, 14 (Autumn 1982).

In virtually all cases, the sogo shosha handle the import, export, offshore, and domestic trade of about 20,000 items. These goods can be divided into six major product groups—general merchandise, metals, energy and chemicals, machinery, textiles, and foodstuffs (see Table 4.2). Since they trade in so diverse a range of products, the sogo shosha have great flexibility in dealing in international markets. Barter trade or counterpurchasing, for instance, is done by the sogo shosha because of their ability to accept manufactured goods, foodstuffs, or other commodities as payment in lieu of hard currency.[25]

To carry out their varied daily activities, the sogo shosha maintain extensive worldwide information networks. Not only can few companies anywhere in the world compete with their information-gathering capability but it has been said with some justification that their capability even surpasses that of the CIA. As a whole, the top nine sogo shosha have about 1,100 offices, linked by highly sophisticated telecommunications systems, in some 200 cities around the world.

The American exporter who wishes to export to Japan but not incur a heavy investment should consider using a capable trading company to act as distributor. One great advantage in using a trading company that the potential exporter should keep in mind is that most trading companies work on volume. The amount charged by the trading company to the exporter or importer is usually relatively small.

In picking a trading company to act as distributor, some points that the potential exporter should keep in mind are:

(1) Size—over the years it has been true that if a product requires a high degree of skill in marketing, planning for promotional programs, and other sophisticated marketing activities, specialized trading companies are generally the most effective. This generalization, though, is not true for every product, especially since many sogo shosha have set up separate trading companies to deal with products requiring more specialized skills. The best advice appears to be to investigate the product strengths and skills of both the sogo shosha and smaller trading companies.

(2) Adequacy of distribution—the potential exporter should certainly investigate the experience of the company and its staff in handling the goods. If the trading company already handles a competitor's products, a major issue is whether separate staff will be assigned to sales of one's products or whether there is a strong likelihood of it being given second position to the competitor.

(3) Product experience—the potential exporter should consider the trading company's experience with the exporter's products as well as the trading company's ability to provide sophisticated marketing skills and proper distribution connections.

(4) Ability to provide finance—although overseas exporters often finance some product exports to Japan on their own account, if financing

Table 4.2
Percentage Breakdown of Annual Turnover of Nine Sogo Shosha, 1978

Firm	Metals	Machinery	Chemicals	Foods	Textiles	Fuel	Projects, Pulp & Lumber
Mitsubishi	28	18	9	13	5	18	9
Mitsui	31	19	12	14	6	7	11
C. Itoh	17	20	20	13	19	6	5
Marubeni	24	26	12	14	13	2	9
Sumitomo	33	25	19	9	4	2	9
Nissho-IOwai	36	25	11	10	8	3	7
Kanematsu	19	12	13	15	28	13	—
Tomen	21	19	15	19	20	2	4
Nichimen	22	23	11	15	19	4	6

Source: Y. Tsurumi, *Sogoshosha—Engines of Export-Based Growth* (1980).

in Japan is desired, the potential exporter should certainly evaluate the credit worthiness and borrowing power of the proposed trading company.

(5) Group affiliation—the group membership of the trading company being considered should be investigated, and before a deal is actually concluded, it should be made clear as to whether dealing with a particular trading company will imply working exclusively with other members of the group. Ties with group trading companies can have the advantage of providing access to banking, insurance, and other companies in the group on more favorable terms. On the other hand, close ties with one group might foreclose opportunities to deal with firms in other groups. The question of group affiliation is primarily an issue in the case of large trading firms, since smaller ones are usually more independent.

(6) Exclusivity—there are two questions of exclusivity involved in dealing with trading companies: (1) whether the potential exporter overseas will deal exclusively with one trading company, and (2) whether that trading company will deal only in the products of the overseas exporter. It is not uncommon to find large trading companies dealing in competing products, although they generally assign different persons to be in charge of sales. The precise method in which products will be handled is an important question to raise, since product conflicts might reduce the chances for success.

Information on which trading companies deal in various products is available from the trade index published by the Japan Chamber of Commerce, as well as from the Japan Import Association and various industry associations. In addition, the U.S. Department of Commerce maintains a list of importers in Japan as well as information on market research companies with operations in Japan. These latter companies can often be used to advantage to sift through various possible candidates for importer or partner in Japan and then assist in the selection of an appropriate company.

Trading companies in Japan receive a large number of inquiries in foreign languages, but normally only the largest trading firms have the staff to answer all the letters received. Even then, the criteria for selection usually include a certain minimum level of sales per year in the case of large trading firms. For this reason, information must be sufficiently detailed to provoke interest. After a list of potential trading company candidates has been compiled, letters may be sent, but they should be accompanied by basic information on the sales, capitalization, and other accounting data on the potential exporter as well as detailed product catalogues. Since letters do not always reach the most appropriate individual, a potential exporter should not give up with one mailing. As I mentioned earlier, many trading companies have offices in the United States and can be contacted there.

Table 4.3 shows the organization of a large general trading company. As the figure suggests, most trading companies are organized by product. Thus, if an American company wishes to contact a large general trading company by letter, the division in charge of the product to be exported should receive the letter, with a copy sent to the public relations department as well.

One point that should not be overlooked by Americans is the new role the sogo shosha are playing. Many of them are mobilizing their vast resources for the development of new enterprises, new products and services, and even new technologies. The objective is not for the large trading companies to become manufacturing ones; it is rather to develop new businesses for which the trading company can render marketing and other services in which it has expertise. Most of the large trading companies to assure both the development of and a continuing relationship with these new businesses now even provide such venture capital as may be necessary on a case-by-case basis.[26]

Another way for an American company to export its product or technology to Japan is through a licensing agreement. In a licensing agreement, the maker of goods or the owner of a technological process "licenses" another party to make the goods or use this process. Commonly, the licensor is paid both a fee and a percentage of the sales or the profit of the licensee. Until the 1970s, the importation of foreign technology through licensing agreements played a major role in the development of the Japanese economy. From 1950 to 1969, for example, Japan paid $2,147 million to foreign nations as royalties for imported technology while receiving only $180 million for exported assistance; in other words, royalties paid to Japanese companies during this period were only 8.4 percent of royalties paid to foreign companies.[27] Although this gap has narrowed considerably since then, it should be noted that the paid royalties in 1976 ($846 million) were the biggest annual payment since 1950.[28] Japan still is an important market for foreign industries desiring returns from the technology they have developed.

Japanese antitrust law will be discussed in much more detail in chapter 7, but for now it should be mentioned that Japanese antitrust law must be carefully studied by the potential licensor. The Japanese Antimonopoly Act, which regulates monopolies using patents and unfair business practices resulting from licensing agreements, prohibits any international private agreement or contract (such as a licensing agreement) involving an undue restraint of trade or an unfair trade practice and requires that *all* international licensing agreements within thirty days of their execution be registered with the Japanese Fair Trade Commission (JFTC) for screening.[29] In May 1968, the JFTC issued guidelines as to what types of restrictive clauses in licensing agreements are illegal in Japan (a copy of these guidelines is attached as Appendix A to this chapter).[30]

Table 4.3
Organization of a Major Trading Company

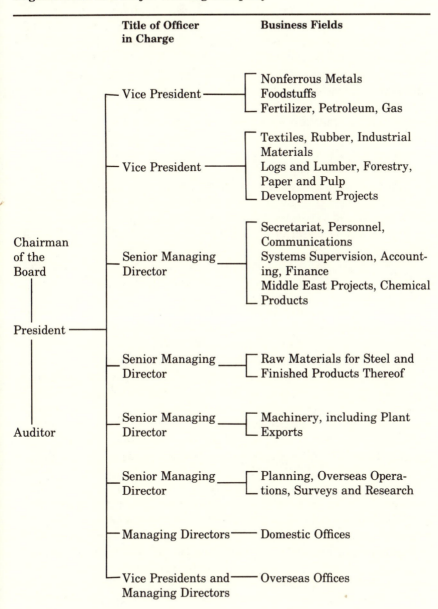

	Title of Officer in Charge	Business Fields
Chairman of the Board	Vice President	Nonferrous Metals Foodstuffs Fertilizer, Petroleum, Gas
	Vice President	Textiles, Rubber, Industrial Materials Logs and Lumber, Forestry, Paper and Pulp Development Projects
	Senior Managing Director	Secretariat, Personnel, Communications Systems Supervision, Accounting, Finance Middle East Projects, Chemical Products
President	Senior Managing Director	Raw Materials for Steel and Finished Products Thereof
Auditor	Senior Managing Director	Machinery, including Plant Exports
	Senior Managing Director	Planning, Overseas Operations, Surveys and Research
	Managing Directors	Domestic Offices
	Vice Presidents and Managing Directors	Overseas Offices

Source: Japan External Trade Organization (JETRO), *The Role of Trading Companies in International Commerce*, JETRO Marketing Series 2, 29 (1980).

At the end of 1979 in response to foreign pressure, the Japanese government amended the law regarding foreign investment and foreign exchange in Japan.[31] The amendment radically changed the principle of foreign investment in Japan: before, foreign investment in Japan was usually prohibited unless specifically allowed while after the amendment the situation was reversed. Although the 1979 amendment is primarily concerned with foreign exchange and trade, parts of it do affect licensing agreements. In many cases now, although the American licensor must file a report in advance of the agreement with both the Bank of Japan and the Japanese ministry with jurisdiction over the field of the agreement, their approval is not required. In other cases, though, especially those involving licensing agreements in such fields as computers and laser processing, the Bank of Japan will not issue an approval if the Japanese ministry concerned issues a notice to withhold approval.[32] The American lawyer or businessman involved is strongly urged to consider the effect of this recent amendment before beginning any negotiations with the Japanese regarding a licensing agreement.

There are three problems in particular concerning Japan for those Americans contemplating marketing their product or technology through the vehicle of a licensing agreement. One problem is the pervasive influence of the Japanese government in this area. As we saw earlier, the JFTC must approve all international licensing agreements. In addition, the august presence of the Ministry of International Trade and Industry (MITI) looms as large here as it seemingly does over every other facet of the Japanese economy.[33] Most license agreements must be approved by MITI, and the agency takes its responsibility of safeguarding Japan's economic interests seriously.[34] If one negotiates with a prospective licensee without taking account of MITI's eventual participation in the licensing process, one may find oneself in what appears to be an entirely new round of negotiation after the license has seemingly been settled. The length of the license term, provisions for field of use grants, cross-license considerations, royalty rates, considerations relative to patents and know-how, participation in after-developed technology, joint research and development, and other fundamentals of most license negotiations are all of concern to MITI, depending in part upon the industry and the state of the licensee's own technology. In addition, there remain policies regarding "prototypes"— where one may be permitted to sell directly the first installation of a new product only upon condition of licensing the technology for home exploitation thereafter—government procurement standards, advance "committee work" on "safety" standards, and a host of other such considerations that can have a highly practical effect upon whether a license will be permitted or the extent to which it will operate to the licensor's actual advantage.

Another problem for the American company contemplating licensing its technology to a Japanese entity is that the American company is disclosing its secrets to a potential competitor. Once the agreement ends, the Japanese company will have knowledge of the technology and may very well become a competitor.

The other problem particularly applicable to licensing agreements entered into with the Japanese arises out of the judgment of the Tokyo High Court[35] in 1971 in a suit sought by Novo Industry, Ltd., a Danish company, against the Japan Fair Trade Commission for the nullification of a JFTC order issued against the Japanese company Amano Pharmaceutical Co., Ltd.[36] Although this case involved a distributorship agreement, its holding and influence are also directly applicable to licensing agreements.

As was briefly discussed earlier in this chapter, the Japanese Antimonopoly Act prohibits any international licensing agreement involving an undue restraint of trade or unfair business practice and also requires that all international licensing agreements be registered within thirty days of execution with the JFTC. Under this statute, an entrepreneur is prohibited from entering into an agreement which contains terms pertaining to an unfair business practice, irrespective of whether he is the active or passive party to the practice.[37] If an American licensor, for example, imposes under the licensing agreement an unfair business practice against a Japanese party, the JFTC may order the Japanese party to abandon or cancel the agreement by which he was compelled to accept this unfair business practice. Thus, the Japanese licensee will in fact benefit from a JFTC order issued against himself by reason of a violation of Article 6 of the Antimonopoly Act: the Japanese party will have learned, pursuant to the licensing agreement, how to make the goods or use the technology process—and yet by order of the JFTC the Japanese party will no longer be bound to the licensing agreement which in all likelihood prevents him from using the technology learned for a period of years after the agreement ends. The matter involving Amano and Novo was just such a case.

Amano, a Japanese manufacturer and seller of pharmaceutical products, and Novo, a Danish manufacturer and seller of pharmaceutical products, in June of 1966 entered into a distributorship agreement relating to certain enzymatic products of Novo in Japan. Amano, however, failed to register the distribution agreement with the JFTC within 30 days of its execution as it is required to do under Article of the Antimonopoly Act; in fact, Amano did not register the agreement with the JFTC in 1966 at all.

At the end of 1969, Novo terminated the distributorship agreement. In that year, Amano finally submitted to the JFTC a copy of the agreement.[38] After discussing the matter with Amano and examining the agreement itself, the JFTC declared that three provisions of the agreement infringed the statute prohibiting unfair business practices. On December 16, 1969, the JFTC ordered Amano to abandon the provisions which prohibited it from manufacturing, selling, and otherwise handling products which competed with those to which the distributorship agreement related—even after termination of the agreement.[39] Novo was not consulted at all.[40] Amano consented in writing to the decree, glad to be able to do so since it could now violate with impunity the contract's provisions preventing it from handling any product which would compete with those in the distributorship agreement. Novo, though, appealed the decision to the Tokyo High Court.

Though Novo argued against the JFTC decision as to the legality of the provisions of the agreement under the antitrust law, the most critical issue in the litigation was whether Novo had the right to bring proceedings in court against a JFTC order which technically had not been issued against it but rather against Amano, i.e., whether or not Novo had "standing." The Tokyo High Court dismissed the action, ruling that Novo had no right to bring proceedings aginst the JFTC in relation to the order issued against Amano; at best, the Court held, Novo was only "indirectly" affected by the order. Novo did appeal this decision to the Japanese Supreme Court, but without success.[41]

The *Novo* decision is an important one for foreigners interested in licensing use of their technology or products to the Japanese. Unless the agreement is exempted by Article 6(3) of the Japanese Antimonopoly Act, the foreign party who is going to enter into an agreement with a Japanese party must see that the agreement is drafted so as not to involve any unfair business practice or undue restraint of trade. In addition, the foreign party must make sure that the agreement is registered with the Japanese government within thirty days of its execution. Otherwise, the result may be analogous to that in the *Novo* decision, a case in which ironically the Japanese defendant hoped that a JFTC decision would be issued against it. The decision voided parts of the licensing agreement and thereby allowed the Japanese party to manufacture, sell, and handle products which would compete with those in the distributorship agreement, even though these acts were prohibited by the agreement itself. This case was a rarity in the law: the defendant by having a judgment handed down against it actually emerged victorious. The real defendant, the foreign company, was held to be powerless to intervene in the matter.

Another vehicle for doing business in Japan is through a joint-venture. A joint venture is commonly composed of a company incorporated under Japanese law by the joint investment of a foreign investor(s) and a Japanese investor(s) and managed by both. The advantages of a joint venture are that it makes it possible for a foreign company seeking to enter the Japanese market to limit business risks and thus reduce costs (by sharing them with the Japanese partner), facilitates the creation of an enterprise with a size sufficient to penetrate an already existing market, and allows the reciprocal exchange of technology and resources.[42] Joint ventures are a means by which both sides can share capital and risk and make use of each other's technical strength. For the American company contemplating entering into a joint venture with a Japanese partner, another possible way both to enter the Japanese market and to have a cognizable presence there is by establishing a wholly owned subsidiary or a branch of the company there. An advantage of the joint venture scheme, though, is that if the company's competitors are well established in Japan, the foreigner's partner's knowledge of the domestic Japanese market may be of great help. In addition, if barriers (tariff or otherwise) or other marketing problems exist which make the foreign investor's business difficult, the local participation in the joint venture in terms of capital, labor, and other factors may facilitate the obtaining of cooperation from governmental agencies, banks, and private business, thus enhancing the prospects for expansion and development.

The American considering a joint venture agreement should keep in mind during the negotiations of the agreement that a joint venture can succeed only through the cooperation of both parties. Since both will jointly manage the business and share interests and responsibilities, they need to establish a strong relationship and to be bound together by commonality of interest. A difference in opinion between them can make management of a joint venture difficult. To avert such situations, a 50-50 split of control should be avoided; otherwise, a difference of opinion may lead to non-resolution of problems.

For the joint venture to succeed, the American should make sure that the following points are satisfied before the execution of the agreement:

(1) The suitability of the Japanese partner—some points to be considered by the American in evaluating the suitability of his partner are the business scale of the Japanese, the reputation and prestige of the Japanese company in Japan, the business philosophy of the Japanese company, and its future objectives. [43](2) The short- and long-term business plans of each partner—the objectives of the joint venture should be compatible with both the short- and long-term plans and strategy of each partner. (3) The possibility of doing business through a medium other than the joint venture agreement—each party should examine whether any method other than the joint-venture agreement is better for each party's individual purpose and goal and the mutual

ones. Sometimes, for example, a licensing agreement may be preferable for the American company in that there is less capital to be invested.

Another way for an American to do business in Japan is by the establishment of a subsidiary. The use of a subsidiary involves great risk for the American—but also protects his technology the most and is the way for him to reap the most success if his product sells well. A subsidiary is a company totally controlled by the parent; in our context the subsidiary in Japan would be owned by the American company.[44]

Until the early 1970s, the establishment of a subsidiary in Japan by a foreign company was subject to strict scrutiny.[45] Largely in response to foreign pressure, though, the regulations regarding the establishment of a subsidiary in Japan by a foreign investor have been greatly liberalized. Whereas until recent years the tenor of the Japanese business law system was to prohibit foreign investment unless specifically allowed by statute, the situation as we saw earlier has now become totally reversed. Today, the Japanese business law system in principle stipulates freedom of foreign exchange, and foreign investment is now allowed unless specifically prohibited.[46]

On December 1, 1980, the Foreign Exchange and Foreign Trade Control Law (the FECL) and its implementing regulations became effective in Japan.[47] The FECL is the statute in Japan directly governing the establishment of a company in Japan by a foreigner.[48] The provisions of the FECL are based on the general principle that all external transactions (a term which encompasses direct investment) should be free of control unless an "emergency" or special exception is deemed to apply. A written contract, for example, formerly required to accompany the application to the Japanese government for approval, is no longer needed; neither is there now a need to translate an English-language version into Japanese.[49]

Under the FECL, the holding of corporate shares by foreigners is classified into three categories: (1) portfolio investment; (2) direct domestic investment; and (3) takeovers. Direct domestic investment is the relevant category for those Americans thinking of establishing a subsidiary in Japan.

Under the FECL, "approval" is no longer ordinarily necessary for a foreign investor to establish a subsidiary in Japan. No more, though, than three months prior to the date of the transaction made for the purpose of establishing a branch, subsidiary, or majority-owned joint venture, the foreign investor must give advance notice of his plans to the Minister of Finance and the minister having jurisdiction over the industry involved.[50] The notice must, *inter alia*, set forth the name, address, nationality, and occupation of the foreign investor (in the case of a juridical person or other organization, the name, principal office address, type of business operations, and amount of capital of the organization); the purpose of the business relating to such investment; the time of consummation of the investment; and the reason for making the investment.[51] A foreign investor is prohibited from going forward with the investment for a period of thirty days after giving such notice, although the waitng period may be decreased in ordinary cases to as little as two weeks.[52]

During the waiting period, the ministers have an opportunity to investigate the investment for any adverse impact it may have.[53] In making this investigation, the ministers are required to consider whether the investment (1) will endanger national security, hinder the maintenance of public order, or hamper the protection of public safety[54] (2) will have a significant adverse effect on the activities of Japanese enterprises in the same or related industries or impede the "smooth operation" of the Japanese economy[55] (3) should be modified or suspended for reasons of mutuality vis-a-vis a nation with which Japan has no treaty obligations regarding restrictions on direct investments[56] or (4) should be modified or suspended because the Minister of Finance has decided to protect the balance of payments, the Japanese yen, or financial and capital markets in Japan by requiring governmental permission for that kind of capital transfer.[57] During the thirty-day period if the ministers determine that further inquiry is necessary, they can extend the waiting period to four months.[58]

If the ministers believe that the proposed investment falls under one of these four criteria, they must refer the matter for advice to the Foreign Exchange Inquiry Council, persons of "academic experience" appointed by the Minister of Finance.[59] If the ministers remain firm in their belief after talking with the Council, they can "suggest" that the transaction be changed or they will suspend its execution.[60] The foreign investor has ten days to tell the ministers whether or not he agrees to comply with their changes.[61] If he does agree, the modified transaction may proceed immediately. If he does not, the ministers have the power to order its change—or even its cancellation.[62]

The foreign investor should realize the significance of the FECL. The establishment of a branch, joint venture, or wholly owned subsidiary now in the usual case is done by a relatively quick and easy procedure. As of the time this book went to press, the Japanese government had used the FECL to open the opportunities for foreign investment in Japan. The government at the moment has dealt with direct foreign investment liberally except in areas deemed by the Japanese government to be "primary industries," namely, agriculture; forest and fisheries; mining and petroleum; and leather manufacturing.[63]

The American seeking to market in Japan a product already successful in the United States should take steps as soon as possible to protect his trademark right (instructions on how to register a trademark in Japan are given in Appendix B to this chapter). The procedure in this area in Japan is radically different from that in the United States and, as one commentator has written, "for the unprepared, Japan can be a business nightmare."[64] In the United States, one can apply for trademark protection only after using the word(s) and/or symbol(s) in actual commerce.[65] In Japan, on the other hand, the first party to apply for a trademark usually ends up owning it. A trademark right in Japan can be created only by registration. The basic principle in Japan is that the first one to file a trademark is entitled to registration.[66]

Japanese law does not, therefore, require prior use for the application or registration of a trademark. In addition, the law allows the use by different owners of the same trademark in thirty-four separate classes of goods for which trademarks in Japan can be registered.[67] In Japan goods for trademark registration purposes are classified by the type of shop that would sell them. If a company applies for a trademark in one class and not another, anyone else can apply for the same trademark in the non-applied-for classes of goods.

It is strongly recommended that a foreign company thinking of marketing its product in Japan not only file as soon as possible to protect its trademark for particular goods but that the company also file to protect its trademark (or a similar one) in classes of goods even tangentially related to their business. The reasons for taking these steps are two-fold: to defend against infringement and also to anticipate possible future use. Coca-Cola, for example, has been frustrated in its Japanese operations because Japanese companies have registered the use of this trademark for the labelling of T-shirts, ashtrays, and other items.[68]

The case of McDonald's, the famous hamburger company, is a legendary one in Japan and proves the value of the axiom: file trademark registrations at once in Japan.[69] Over ten years ago McDonald's lawyers attempted to file to protect its trademarks on the famed golden arches and the name McDonald's. The day before, however, the Japanese food supplier Marushin had applied for those trademarks.[70] McDonald's filed suit to protect its trademark; the case is still unresolved.[71]

Japan's unfair competition law does permit the foreign owner of a trademark to stop its unauthorized registration if the foreign company can satisfy three standards: (1) the trademark is the company's; (2) the trademark is well known in Japan (the fact that the trademark is well known elsewhere in the world is unimportant; it must be well known in Japan); and (3) its use by the other company would cause confusion among consumers.[72] Under the unfair competition law, the foreign company if successful is entitled to a cease-and-desist order against the other side and damages (if any). If, though, the other company has been granted trademark registration rights by filing, it is protected.

Those Americans thinking of doing business in Japan may wish to consider the effect to them of two recent events that have gone largely unnoticed in the West. The first is a series of measures announced on May 27, 1982, by the Japanese government and aimed at increasing the access of foreigners to its capital markets.[73] New guidelines issued by the Ministry of Finance will permit major banks in Japan to lend capital to United States corporations not just to finance trade with Japan but also for general corporate purposes. The new guidelines open the Japanese credit markets to small U.S. companies formerly closed out of them.[74]

There are strong incentives for U.S. companies to tap the Japanese credit markets. The Japanese capital markets are among the best in the world: Japan has a high savings rate, a major role in world trade, and a strong balance of payments. In addition, Japan has for years had a markedly low interest rate. Thus those Americans contemplating doing business in Japan might very well finance this act not through American capital markets but rather those of Japan.[75] A noteworthy incident in this regard as this book was being written was the announcement by Walt Disney Productions that it had received a cash loan from Japanese banks, the first American company to do so.[76] Although American companies have previously raised funds in Japan, the borrowings have always been in the form of bonds. The precedent set by the Japanese banks' loan to Disney is the potentially significant opening of the Japanese financial market to foreign firms.

The second important event was the establishment in the spring of 1982 by the Japanese government of the Office of the Trade Ombudsman (OTO) to help facilitate the entry of foreign products into Japan. In over 25 percent of the cases referred to it so far by complaining foreigners, the OTO took specific action to smooth the way for the imported product.[77] In one case, for example, an American-made "honey wine" that had been kept out of Japan because it didn't fall into any established product category was allowed to enter the Japanese market after it was classified by the OTO as a "fruit brandy".[78]

A surprising aspect of the OTO is that for all the publicity in the United States about the closed nature of the Japanese market to imports, the OTO has been relatively unused by American exporters with complaints. Those who have taken advantage of its services, though, are not unhappy. One American company, for example, was widely quoted as being "very encouraged" by the way the OTO handled its complaint.[79] An American who believes there are obstacles to the entrance of his product into the Japanese market may very well profit by filing a complaint with the OTO. A recent change permits a grievance to be filed by proxy; no longer must a complaining party be physically present in Japan to take advantage of the OTO.[80]

Those Americans contemplating opening a business in Japan should not concentrate their inquiries solely on the Tokyo area. More and more prefectural governments in Japan are doing their best to persuade foreigners to open their plants in provincial towns and cities. MITI has taken the lead in encouraging local governments in Japan to direct their efforts in this direction, and the governments' reaction has been an enthusiastic one.[81] Many of the prefectural governments use incentive packages to help recruit business. Tax incentives are offered, and applications for government permits are pushed through quickly. Other factors that make the rural areas of Japan attractive to foreigners are the low cost of land and labor compared to Tokyo.[82] In addition, a vastly improved transportation system (including an ever-increasing highway network, improved airports, and frequent high speed trains) makes operating in any part of Japan easier. Such Japanese companies as Sony, Nippon Electric Company (NEC), Canon, and TDK Electronics Company and such American businesses as Texas Instruments and Materials Research have now opened plants far from Tokyo.[83] A foreigner thinking of opening a business in Japan is advised to consider seriously locating the business in a site other than the Tokyo-Osaka area (a 250-mile corridor where one in two Japanese lives).[84]

A difficult barrier, but a surmountable one, for foreign businesses in Japan is hiring good Japanese staff. Hiring domestic talent, though, is a must in Japan for several reasons. One is that the Japanese place a premium on long-term relationships, and they invariably believe that foreign firms will only do business there for a short term; therefore, a crucial expression of commitment to the Japanese market is the hiring of local people. In addition, the complex intricacies of the Japanese business law system, the difficulty of communicating effectively in the Japanese language, and the differences in taste between American and Japanese consumers are just some of the factors that make doing business in Japan frustrating for a foreigner. Local people can help the foreign company cope with these nuances.

The foreign company in Japan seeking to hire local people faces severe problems. The Japanese traditional distrust of foreigners, the rare use in Japan of executive "head-hunters," the lifetime employment system with its many fringe benefits, and the cradle-to-grave paternalism of the system make it difficult for foreign companies to compete effectively in the hiring process.

For the foreign company to be able to hire competent natives, it must begin to recruit them at the university level—as the Japanese companies do. Graduates of such prestigious universities as Tokyo (often referred to by the Japanese as "Todai"), Keio, Waseda, and Kyoto are recruited as early as a year before graduation. Foreign companies must also recruit at that level. In a land such as Japan where people rarely, if ever, change jobs, recruitment any later will almost surely be fruitless.[85]

One area of recruitment that should be emphasized by a foreign firm in Japan is women. Few Japanese companies employ them in a professional role.[86] A foreign company offering to women a greater challenge could be very successful in its recruitment quest. Although opportunities for women in Japan have greatly improved in recent years, they still constitute an underused source of talent. Use of that source intelligently by a foreign company could pay the company enormous dividends in the future.

A common mistake committed by foreign firms in Japan is equating the ability of a Japanese to speak English with his business competence. The two skills are dissimilar and should not be confused by the foreigner. What the foreign competitor in the Japanese market wants to hire is superior talent. The ability of a Japanese to speak English is one index of this talent; it is not, though, the only determinant.

NOTES

1. This statement is true even in the area of television programming. "The Winds of War" and "Dallas" are two programs that were immense rating successes in the United States. In Japan, on the other hand, the shows' ratings were disastrous. Sam Jameson, "'Dallas': A Dry Hole in Japan," *The Los Angeles Times*, June 12, 1983, "Calendar," at 6.

2. For a good analysis of how to market successfully in Japan, see *Marketing in Japan* (R. Ballon ed. 1974).

3. *See* Terry Trucco, "Serving Mr. Donut and the Community," *The New York Times*, December 26, 1982, Section 3 (Business), at 6. The two largest foreign-begun, fast-food businesses in Japan are McDonald's and Kentucky Fried Chicken.

4. The head of Mister Donut in Japan, Keiji Chiba, has said that "all we use from the American community is the logo." *Id.* at 7.

5. The most recent is *U.S. Opportunities to Japan*, published in August of 1978. Although the book is somewhat out of date (especially its market survey information), the potential exporter will find within it valuable information on Japanese marketing characteristics and on the mechanics of importing and distributing in Japan.

6. At last count there were thirteen state and seventeen port authority offices in Tokyo.

7. The ACCJ also takes an active role in discussions of bilateral trade issues.

8. Those advertising in the *ACCJ Journal* that they provide assistance in Japan to American companies are generally only American firms. On the other hand, Japanese publications usually list only Japanese consultants.

9. The Keidanren is, in fact, so prominent that its president has often been

referred to as the prime minister of Japan's "invisible government." *See, e.g.,* D. Henderson, *Foreign Enterprise in Japan* 57 (1973).

10. The American headquarters of each one is located in New York City.

11. Commercial Code, Art. 479.

12. Statement of Senator Stevenson, Chairman of the Subcommittee on International Finance, Committee on Banking (August 27, 1980).

13. *See, e.g.,* Y. Tsurumi, *Sogoshosha—Engines of Export-Based Growth* 1 (1980). Until the enactment of the Export Trading Act of 1982, American trading companies were prohibited by antitrust and banking laws.

14. Export Trading Act of 1982, Pub. L. No. 97-290, 96 Stat. 1233 (1982). For a good analysis of the law, *see* Donald Baker, "The Export Trading Company Act: An Amalgam of Competing Ideas," *The National Law Journal,* January 17, 1983, at 21.

15. H. Report No. 97-637, Part I 2431-2432, 97th Cong., 2nd Sess. (1982).

16. *See, e.g.,* Sam Jameson, "Mitsubishi Casts Doubt on U.S. Exporting Plan," *The Los Angeles Times,* February 21, 1982, Part V (Business), at 1.

17. Professor Tsurumi of the UCLA Graduate School of Management has called them "the engines of the export-based economic growth of Japan." Y. Tsurumi, *supra* note 13, at ix. Another writer has described the trading company as "a Japanese institution". Jameson, *supra* note 16, at 1.

18. *See, e.g.,* Masayoshi Kanabayashi, "Japan's Big and Evolving Trade Firms: Can the U.S. Use Something Like Them?" *The Wall Street Journal,* December 17, 1980, at 48.

19. Japan External Trade Organization (JETRO), *The Role of Trading Companies in International Commerce,* JETRO marketing series 2, 5 (1980).

20. *See, e.g.,* Cappiello, "The Changing Role of Japan's General Traders," 1 *Journal of Japanese Trade and Industry* 18, 19 (July 1982).

21. Dziubla, "International Trading Companies: Building on the Japanese Model," 4 *Nw. J. Int'l L. & Bus.* 422, 423 (1982).

22. Cappiello, *supra* note 20, at 19.

23. In 1979, for example, the nine largest sogo shosha accounted for 54.5 percent of Japan's imports and 48.2 percent of other imports. Kanabayashi, *supra* note 18, at 48.

24. Cappiello, *supra* note 20, at 19.

25. The ability of the sogo shosha to accept goods as payment instead of money has recently become a valuable asset. Barter in international trade is becoming more and more prevalent, especially in Southeast Asia. *See,* "Going Under the Counter," *Far Eastern Economic Review,* January 27, 1983, at 49.

26. Mitsubishi, for instance, has an aerospace team organized specifically to direct the marketing of the gas turbine newly manufactured by United Technologies Corp., an American company. In another case, Mitsubishi has provided funds and considerable marketing expertise for the development of overseas markets for the Japanese company Konishiroku's U-Bix copiers. "Sogoshoshas: Total Business Development Not Just Passive Investment," *Far Eastern Economic Review,* December 3, 1982, at 74.

27. Yoshio Kumakura, "Licensing," in 4 *Doing Business in Japan* VI 6-3 (Z. Kitagawa ed. 1982).

28. *Id.,* at VI 6-4.

29. Antimonopoly and Fair Trade Maintenance Act (Antimonopoly Act) (Shiteki Dokusen no Kinshi Oyobi Kosei Torihi ni Kansuru Horitsu), Art. 6 (Law No. 54, April 14, 1947).

30. Antimonopoly Act Guidelines for International Licensing Agreements, issued by the Fair Trade Commission on May 24, 1968.

31. The Law Partially Amending the Foreign Exchange and Foreign Trade Control Law (Law No. 65, 1979). For an excellent translation, *see JASLS Reports—Newsletter of the Japanese American Society for Legal Studies, American Branch*, Issue No. 1 (Anderson trans. 1980).

32. *See, e.g.*, Ohba, "Recent Changes in the Foreign Exchange Control Law and the Law Concerning Foreign Investment in Japan," *The International Contract—Law and Finance Review 1980 Yearbook* 181-183 (1981).

33. For a good analysis of how MITI has dominated the Japanese business scene since World War II, *see* C. Johnson, *MITI and the Japanese Miracle* (1982).

34. *See, e.g.*, Charles Cohler, "Antitrust Aspects of Licensing in Japan," An Unpublished Paper 8 (1980).

35. The Tokyo High Court, as we saw earlier, is ordinarily a court of appellate jurisdiction, but it has exclusive jurisdiction at first instance over suits brought against JFTC orders. Court Act, Art. 16.

36. *Novo Industry, Ltd. v. Fair Trade Commission*, 17 Kosei Torihiki Iinkai Shinketsushu 297 (Tokyo High Court 1971).

37. *See, e.g.*, Kawamura, "A New Development in Japanese Antitrust Law: Its Application to International Transactions," 3 *Lawasia* 179, 181 (1972).

38. *Nippon Keizai Shimbun [Japan Economic Newspaper]*, December 14, 1969, at 1.

39. J.F.T.C. Consent Decree, Kan No. 22, 1969.

40. Since Novo did not have any physical existence such as a branch office or a liaison representative in Japan, it was entirely excluded from the proceedings before the JFTC. The order was issued only against Amano. Kawamura, *supra* note 37, at 179, 185.

41. 29 Minshu 1592 (S. Ct., 3d P.B., 1975).

42. Joint ventures between foreign and Japanese partners are most common in technical innovation areas. Yukio Yanagida, "Joint Venture," in 4 *Doing Business in Japan* VII 3-1, 3-3 (Z. Kitagawa ed. 1982).

43. Especially in the 1960s, many joint ventures were established in Japan based on conflicting motivations of the parties. Problems inevitably ensued. When the Japanese partner had acquired the needed technology from the foreign company, it frequently began to manifest a desire to use the technology on its own, an act prohibited by the joint-venture agreement. The foreigner, on the other hand, often found that it had not been able to enter the Japanese market as successfully as it had hoped. Instead, the joint-venture agreement had only served to furnish technology to a Japanese company which now was eager to compete with the foreign company. *See, e.g., id.*, at VII 3-7.

44. The parent usually owns the majority of the stock and thus can choose the directors of the subsidiary.

45. The Foreign Investment Law of 1950, for example, prohibited the inflow of foreign capital but made exceptions for selected desired investment. Gaishi ni Kansuru Horitsu (Foreign Investment Law) (Law No. 163, 1950).

46. *See, e.g.*, Michiko Ito Crampe and Nicholas Benes, "Majority Ownership Strategies for Japan," 1 *Pacific Basin L.J.* 41, 43 (1982).

47. Gaikoku Kawase oyobi Gaikoku Boeki Kanri Ho (Foreign Exchange and Foreign Trade Control Law) (Law No. 228 of 1960, as amended by Law No. 65 of 1979). For a complete translation of the FECL, *see JASLS Reports— Newsletter of the Japanese American Society for Legal Studies, American Branch,* Issue No. 1 (Anderson trans., 1980). For an excellent analysis of the FECL, *see* Kaname Seki, "The Amendment of the Foreign Exchange and Foreign Trade Control Law and the Effects Thereof," 2 *The Japan Business Law Journal* 29 (February 1981).

48. *See, e.g.*, Nobuyuki Konaka, "Subsidiary," in 4 *Doing Business in Japan* VII 2-1, 2-6 (Z. Kitagawa ed. 1982).

49. Tatsuta, "Restrictions on Foreign Investment: Developments in Japanese Law," 3 *J. of Comp. Corp. Law and Sec. Reg.* 159 (1981).

50. FECL, *supra* note 47, Art. 26(3). Usually, the latter would be the Minister of International Trade and Industry.

51. Tainai Chokusetsu Toshinado ni Kansuru Seirei (Cabinet Order Concerning Direct Domestic Investment), Art. 2(12) (Cabinet Order No. 261 of 1980).

52. FECL, *supra* note 47, Art. 26(4).

53. *Id.*, Art. 27.

54. *Id.*, Art. 27(1)(i).

55. *Id.*, Art. 27(1)(ii).

56. *Id.*, Art. 27(1)(iii).

57. *Id.*, Art. 27(1)(iv).

58. *Id.*, Art. 27(1). If the Foreign Exchange Inquiry Council so requests, the waiting period can be lengthened to a total of five months. *Id.*, Art. 27(3).

59. *Id.*, Art. 27(2).

60. *Id.*, Art. 55-3(2). This "recommendation" is a form of administrative guidance, a practice unique to Japan which will be discussed in Chapter 6.

61. *Id.*, Art. 27(4).

62. *Id.*, Art. 27(7).

63. *See, e.g.*, Tatsuta, *supra* note 49, at 358.

64. "Japan Trademarks Can Prove Elusive," *The New York Times*, April 5, 1983, at 32.

65. The Lanham Act, 15 U.S.C. sec. 1051.

66. "Report From Japan: Tips on Trademarks," *International Lawyer's Newsletter* 3 (Summer 1980).

67. "Japan Trademarks Can Prove Elusive," *The New York Times*, April 5, 1983, at 32.

68. *Id.* I have even heard that one enterprising entrepreneur in Japan, a nation whose teenagers it seems love to wear T-shirts with American university names, has registered the name "Harvard Company" for labelling T-shirts. The word "Harvard" on the T-shirts is printed in very large capital letters and the word "Company" in very small print.

69. This story was told to me in Tokyo in the summer of 1981 by Conan P. Grames, Esq.

70. Marushin applied for these trademarks:

McDonald's trademarks are shown below:

McDonald's

McDonald's trademark, with appropriate registration symbols, is used with the permission of McDonald's Corporation, Oak Brook, Illinois.

71. Since the Japanese trademark officials have not yet approved Marushin's applications, McDonald's can still use its name and symbol.

72. Lecture by attorney Conan Grames, as part of the Santa Clara Law School Summer in Tokyo Program during the summer of 1981.

73. *See, e.g.*, Barbara Thomas, "Easing Access to Japanese Capital," *Business Week*, August 30, 1982, at 10, and "Borrowing Yen Will Be Just a Little Bit Easier," *Business Week*, May 31, 1982, at 32.

74. Before the new guidelines, foreign companies seeking money in the Tokyo market had either to prove they were financing specific Japanese exports or to sell so-called Samurai bonds to Japanese institutional investors. The bond market was effectively closed to all but the most creditworthy companies. It was also limited to very large deals—$50 million or more—and confined to just one foreign issuer each quarter. "Borrowing Yen Will Be Just a Little Bit Easier," *Business Week*, May 31, 1982, at 32.

75. There are, of course, negative points to be considered by an American thinking of borrowing money from Japanese banks. One is the usual conservative attitude of Japanese bankers. The complaint is frequently voiced that they lend only to those who don't really need it. Another is the limit put by the Ministry of Finance on the amount of yen individual banks can lend to offshore borrowers, a limit that interestingly enough has not been made public. A third problem to consider is that if the yen significantly appreciates against the dollar between the time the loan is made and it becomes due the loan will become that much more expensive. *Id.*

76. *See. e.g.*, Sam Jameson, "Japan Banks Lend Disney $63 Million," *The Los Angeles Times*, June 20, 1982, Part IV (Business), at 1.

77. One-fourth of the complaints were rejected and the rest are pending. Urban Lehner, "Japan's Trade Ombudsman Helps to Calm Foreign Protests, but New Clouds Appear," *The Wall Street Journal*, August 6, 1983, at 35.

78. *Id.*

79. *Id.*

80. Nakamura, "The Office of Trade Ombudsman," *JEI Report*, No. 13A, April 8, 1983, at 1, 2.

81. *See, e.g.*, Fumiko Mori, "Local Areas in Japan Vie for Foreign Investment," *JEI Report*, No. 13B, April 8, 1983, at 4.

82. *Id.*, at 5.

83. David Carlson, "Japan's Rural Regions Hustle to Attract Foreign Companies," *The Wall Street Journal*, April 26, 1983, at 31.

84. *Id.*

85. In some job areas, job changing is becoming more common. A recent survey showed that 10 percent of recent college graduates in the electronics industry had already changed jobs (a very high figure in Japan). Toshio Wakamatsu, "Foreign Firms Vie for Local Talent in Japan," *The Wall Street Journal*, April 25, 1983, at 26.

86. *See, e.g.*, R. Christopher, *The Japanese Mind* 101-117 (1983).

Antimonopoly Act Guidelines for International Licensing Agreements

May 24, 1968
Fair Trade Commission

1. Among the restrictions which are liable to come under unfair business practices in international licensing agreements on patent rights or utility model rights (hereinafter referred to as "patent rights"), the following are the outstanding:

    (1) To restrict the area to which the license may export the goods covered by patent rights (hereinafter referred to as "patented goods").

    However, cases coming under (a), (b) or (c) listed below are excluded:

    (a) In case the licensor has patent rights which have been registered in the area to which the licensee's export is restricted (hereinafter referred to as "restricted area");

    (b) In case the licensor is selling patented goods in the restricted area in his continuous business;

    (c) In case the licensor has granted to a third party an exclusive license to sell in the restricted area.

    (2) To restrict the licensee's export prices or quantities of patented goods, or to make it obligatory for the licensee to export patented goods through the licensor or a person designated by the licensor.

    However, such cases are excluded where the licensor grants license to export to the area coming under either of the preceding (a), (b) or (c) and the said restrictions or obligations imposed are of reasonable scope.

    (3) To restrict the licensee from manufacturing, using or selling goods, or employing technology which are in competition with the licensed subject.

However, such cases are excluded where the licensor grants an exclusive license and imposes no restriction on goods already being manufactured, used or sold, or technology already being utilized by the licensee.

(4) To make it obligatory for the licensee to purchase raw materials, parts, etc. from the licensor or a person designated by the licensor.

(5) To make it obligatory for the licensee to sell patented goods through the licensor or a person designated by the licensor.

(6) To restrict the resale prices of patented goods in Japan.

(7) To make it obligatory for the licensee to inform the licensor of knowledge or experience newly obtained regarding the licensed technology, or to assign the right with respect to an improved or applied invention by the licensee to the licensor or to grant the licensor a license thereon.

However, such cases are excluded where the licensor bears similar obligations and the obligations of both parties are equally balanced in substance.

(8) To charge royalties on goods which do not utilize licensed technology.

(9) To restrict the quality of raw materials, parts, etc. or of patented goods.

However, such cases are excluded where such restrictions are necessary to maintain the credibility of the registered trademark or to insure the effectiveness of the licensed technology.

2. The aforementioned guidelines shall apply to international know-how licensing agreements.

3. In international licensing agreements on patent rights, etc., the following acts shall be regarded as the exercise of rights under the Patent Act or the Utility Model Act:

(1) To grant license to manufacture, use, sell, etc. separately;

(2) To grant license for a limited period within the life of patent rights or for a limited area within the whole area covered by patent rights, etc.;

(3) To restrict the manufacture of patented goods to a limited field of technology or to restrict the sale thereof to a limited field of sales;

(4) To restrict the use of patented processes to a limited field of technology;

(5) To restrict the amount of output or the amount of sales of patented goods or to restrict the frequency of the use of patented processes.

How to Register a Trademark in Japan

APPENDIX **B**

Time Schedule:

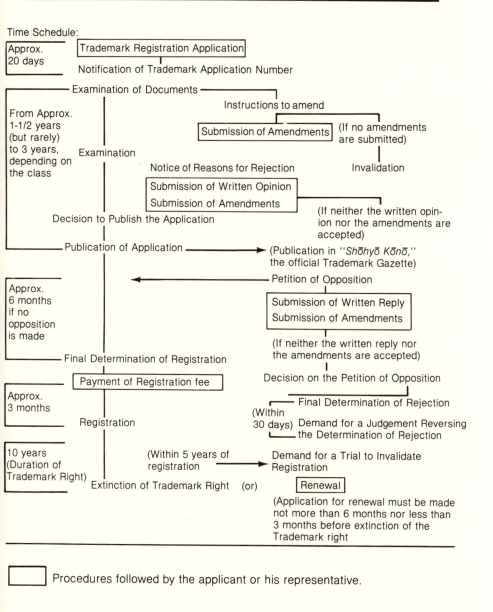

| Procedures followed by the applicant or his representative.

Legal Aspects of Doing Business in Japan   **5**

For the foreigner seeking to do business in Japan, there are several legal issues to consider. Such questions—as do Japanese courts discriminate against foreigners and how expensive is litigation in Japan—are all of primary importance. For an American lawyer interested in the Japanese business law system, such issues as the willingness of Japanese courts to enforce foreign judgments and arbitral awards are equally crucial.

When a foreigner does business in another country, a paramount issue to him is not only what effect the laws of that nation will have on him but also which country's laws will govern his activities. The rules in Japan for determining which country's laws will govern a particular legal transaction which involves at least one non-Japanese party or an act occurring outside of Japan are governed by what the Japanese call "private international law" (a term analogous to what those versed in our legal system would term "choice of law rules"). Used broadly, the phrase encompasses issues of international civil procedure such as the standing of a foreign litigant to sue or be sued in Japan and the enforcement of foreign judgments by Japanese courts. The primary source for such rules in Japan is the Horei (sometimes translated as the "Act Concerning the Application of Law"). The Horei was promulgated in 1889; since then, it has been amended in 1943, 1947, and 1964.

The Horei is an indispensable reference tool for the American lawyer called upon to advise his American client regarding either dealings with a Japanese party or business dealings in Japan. An important issue, for example, concerning the dealings of a foreign company and a Japanese one is which party's nation's law controls if there is a dispute as to the contract's interpretation. The Horei allows the parties themselves to choose which law will govern the validity and effect of such legal acts as the entering into of a contractual agreement.[1] When the parties, however, do fail to specify in the agreement which country's law is to govern, Japanese courts will attempt to determine which law the parties had intended to govern on the basis of the circumstances of their agreement. If such a determination cannot be made, the governing law will be the law of the place where the act was performed.[2] When the contracting parties are from two different countries and the Japanese court is not able to find an express or implied choice of law in the agreement itself, the law that governs is that of the nation from where the offer came. The law of the offeror's domicile governs, if the offeree is unaware from where the offer came when he did accept.[3]

Japanese courts have shown great deference to clauses in contracts ousting them from jurisdiction. This deference is based on the dictates of Article 25 of the Japanese Code of Civil Procedure: "[T]he parties may decide the jurisdictional court by agreement ... The agreement shall not be valid unless it is in writing ..."[4] The deference shown by Japanese courts to such a clause in a contract between Japanese and foreign parties has been so great, in fact, that they have many times ignored the writing requirement of Article 25. In contrast, they have not done so in purely domestic agreements. In a 1965 domestic case, for example, the writing requirement was strictly enforced. A jurisdictional clause on the face of a domestic airplane ticket was held invalid in that case due to the signature requirement, even though the Japanese Ministry of Transportation had authorized such general terms and conditions in air transportation contracts.[5] In a similar case but one involving a foreign party, though, the court stated that since the writing requirement was not necessarily present universally it should not be overemphasized but rather relaxed in international litigation. The clause was upheld even though the writing requirement had not been satisfied.[6]

Even such a threshold issue as whether or not one has legal capacity (e.g., for an individual as to how old he must be before he can sign contracts himself and be liable if he does not perform) is determined by the Horei. As to this question, the answer is that the individual's national law is determinative.[7] Therefore, if an American's domiciliary state law provides that the legal age of capacity is eighteen years, then that age is also his age for legal capacity in Japan. If, though, his national law is more restrictive than Japanese law, then his capacity to perform legal acts in Japan is governed by Japanese law.[8] Legal incompetency is also, as one might expect, governed by the individual's national law.[9] A foreigner with a domicile or residence in Japan may be declared legally incompetent by a Japanese court only if the grounds for such a decree are recognized under both Japanese law[10] and the foreigner's national law.[11] A foreign individual can bring suit in Japan if he is legally competent to do so under both Japanese law and his own national law.[12]

To do business in Japan on a continuous basis, a foreign corporation must comply with the dictates of the Commercial Code. It must, for example, appoint a representative in Japan, establish an office, register with the government, and give public notice of this registration.[13] A foreign corporation cannot engage in business in Japan until it has complied with the requirements just described.[14]

Before 1950, the Japanese Commercial Code had also provided that the existence of a foreign corporation would not be recognized if it had failed to comply with these registration requirements. A foreign corporation that did not comply with the registration requirements thus could not sue in Japan.[15] The statute, though, was amended in 1950. Today, failure of a foreign corporation to satisfy the registration requirements of Japanese law does not impair the foreign corporation's standing to sue in Japan's courts; nor does such a failure affect the validity of a contract made by the foreign corporation. Failure to comply with the registration requirements, though, can give rise to a non-penal fine of not more than ¥300,000 (about $1,300).[16]

As we saw earlier in Chapter 2, much of Japan's law was originally based on that of Germany, a civil law system.[17] Therefore, it should not be surprising to learn that Japan's rules of jurisdiction are virtually identical to those of the German Code of Civil Procedure. The Japanese rules of jurisdiction are for the most part stated in Articles 1-29 of the Japanese Code of Civil Procedure. Their basic principle is that a suit should normally be brought before the court which sits at the domicile of the defendant.[18] Other fora can be the place where the property is located in a suit concerning a property right,[19] the place where the alleged tort occurred in a suit relating to a tort action,[20] and the place where business is conducted if a suit is instituted against a company.[21]

Perhaps the most important Japanese rule of jurisdiction for a foreigner in Japan with no domicile or residence there is the one that states that as long as he has any attachable property in Japan, a court located in the place where the property is located can exercise general jurisdiction over him.[22] The ramifications of this provision are severe for the foreigner in Japan. As long as he has any attachable property whatsoever in Japan, no matter how trivial the value of the property, he can be sued in the court in Japan where the property is located— no matter how large the amount asked by the suer or how tangential the property is to the alleged cause of action. Although the jurisdiction of the Japanese court depends on a finding that the foreign defendant does own some specified property in that area of Japan, the effect of the judgment ultimately rendered by the court is not limited to the value of the property. "In other words," wrote Professor Schlesinger of the German progenitor of the Japanese provision, "the court, having found that defendant owns a piece of local property worth $300, may render a personal judgment against the defendant in the amount of five million dollars."[23] In a paternity case in 1968 brought against the well-known French skier Jean-Claude Killy, for example, involving a provision similar to the Japanese one, an Austrian court based its jurisdiction over defendant Killy on the fact that when leaving Austria he had left a piece of his underwear behind.[24]

Fortunately for foreigners in Japan, the Japanese courts have construed this jurisdictional rule very liberally. Apparently, most Japanese judges believe that this provision should not be applied directly to foreign defendants but rather with reasonable modifications.[25] In *Rosterott v. Admiral Sales Co.*, for example, the Tokyo District Court dismissed an action brought by a salesman against his former employer, a California corporation.[26] The defendant's property in this case was only a few sample goods and a typewriter. The court therefore declared:

If the Code of Civil Procedure Article 8 is to be interpreted to the effect that Japanese jurisdiction extends to an alien-defendant who has any attachable property in Japan, regardless of its nature, quality, or value, the consequence will be very harsh to the defendant not present in Japan.... If the property involved is a tract of land which belongs to the Japanese territory, and if the claim is directly related to the land, the relationship of Japan with the property is sufficient. However, where the property is movable, the relationship is very dim and remote. Attached in this case are, as the plaintiff himself made it clear, a few samples and the like. In addition, since the plaintiff's activities as a salesman in the Far East for the defendant company were not restricted to Japan, it is but by a mere chance that these things are presently in Japan. Such being the case, justice and fairness require us to rule that the relationship of Japan with the property involved is not sufficient to make the exercise of jurisdiction reasonable in light of the fundamental principle.[27]

Another provision of the Japanese Code of Civil Procedure particularly important to foreigners is Article 5. That statute provides that "a suit concerning a property right may be brought before the court situated in the place of performance."[28] In interpreting that clause, Japanese courts have given great weight to the applicable foreign law. In a 1970 case,[29] for instance, the Japanese court ruled it had no jurisdiction over a suit brought by a Japanese creditor against a French debtor because under French law the place to pay damages was the debtor's place of business, France.[30]

Arbitration clauses are common in contracts involving the Japanese.[31] One observer has written that in Japan the "basic attitude toward arbitration is ... assistance and encouragement."[32] In 1950, the Japan Commercial Arbitration Association (JCAA) was established.[33] It is Japan's sole and exclusive agency for the purpose of arbitrating disputes. Its main office is in Tokyo, and it also has branch offices in Yokohama, Nagoya, Kobe, and Osaka.

As of 1979, over sixty countries and regions had arbitration agreements with Japan (a list of those countries is given in Appendix A to this chapter). In addition, Japan was one of the first nations to ratify the Convention on the Recognition and Enforcement of Foreign Arbitral Awards of 1958 (a copy of that convention is contained in Appendix B to this chapter). Provisions in contracts between a Japanese party and a foreigner providing for arbitration will be upheld in Japanese courts regardless of whether the foreign party's country has signed the 1958 Convention or where the place named for arbitration is.[34]

The Japanese attitude toward the enforcement of arbitral clauses is so strong that in one case the Tokyo District Court stated:

Indeed, this agreement provides for arbitration in a foreign country and is made subject to foreign law as regards all aspects concerning formation, validity, and procedure. However, it is reasonable to say that such a foreign arbitration agreement constitutes a bar to a suit brought in violation thereof as does a domestic arbitration agreement under our Code of Civil Procedure.

For, what is the reason our Code recognizes an arbitral agreement as a bar to a suit? The parties have agreed that they do not have recourse to litigation but refer their dispute to arbitrators, private persons, to whose judgment they submit themselves. Such self-settlement of dispute would function to reduce litigation in courts. Therefore, as long as the parties express their desire to rely on arbitration rather than litigation in courts, it is a wise national policy to respect the parties' intent and leave the dispute to their self-settlement. It is a matter of our national policy and has nothing to do with the prestige or power of our judiciary. Hence there is absolutely no necessity to demarcate national boundaries in honoring or rejecting the parties' intent in this regard.[35]

Just as Japan's attitude is highly positive toward the enforcement of arbitral clauses in contracts, so is her attitude toward the enforcement of foreign arbitration awards. Not only has Japan ratified the Convention on the Recognition and Enforcement of Foreign Arbitral Awards of 1958 but her courts have consistently enforced foreign arbitration awards even if the country in which the award was given did not ratify the Convention.[36]

The Convention does state in Article V(2)(6) that a nation may refuse to recognize and enforce a foreign arbitral award if the recognition or enforcement of the award is contrary to the country's public policy. Japanese defendants have often cited this ground as a reason why a Japanese court should refuse to recognize and enforce a foreign arbitral award. Japan's strong policy toward the enforcement of foreign arbitral awards can be seen here since this defense has been consistently rejected by her courts and the awards enforced.[37]

In several cases foreign arbitration awards in favor of foreigners have even been enforced in Japan despite violations of Japan's Foreign Exchange and Foreign Trade Control Law. When these foreigners sought to have the Japanese courts recognize and enforce their award, the Japanese defendants urged the courts to refuse to do so because, they argued, the violation of Japanese law is contrary to Japan's public policy. The Japanese courts, though, have uniformly rejected this defense. In *Fields v. K.K. Taiheiyo T.V.*, for instance, a California judgment confirming an arbitral award was enforced by the Tokyo District Court despite such a public policy argument.[38] The defendant, a Japanese telefilm dealer, and a California corporation called National Telefilm Associates, Inc. (NTA) in March of 1963 entered into a licensing agreement which provided that the Japanese entity would pay to NTA a royalty fee of $13,350 by February of 1964. The Japanese party then sold the film telecast rights to Fuji TV. This type of agreement requires, pursuant to the Foreign Exchange and Foreign Trade Control Law, a license to be issued by the Ministry of Finance; in addition, royalty payments must be made according to the license's terms. The Ministry of Finance at that time granted such licenses directly to the television broadcasting company and not to a broker like the defendant dealer here.[39] The defendant, however, depicted the transaction in the application for the license as if the licensing agreement had actually been negotiated between NTA and Fuji TV. The defendant in the name of Fuji paid to NTA the royalty amount. Before payment, though, the contract had been assigned to the plaintiff by NTA; therefore, the plaintiff should have been paid the royalty. NTA did not transfer the royalty to the plaintiff, and the plaintiff demanded that the defendant pay the royalty amount a second time, but this time to the plaintiff. Pursuant to the arbitral clause in the licensing agreement, the claim went to arbitration. The plaintiff won and brought an action in Japan to have it recognized.

In the enforcement action in Japan, the defendant argued that since the licensing agreement had not been done in compliance with the Foreign Exchange and Foreign Trade Control Law, the California judgment confirming the award was based on an illegal agreement and therefore was contrary to Japan's public policy and should not be recognized and enforced by Japanese courts. Displaying an attitude strongly favorable to the recognition and enforcement of foreign arbitral awards, an attitude typical of Japanese courts, the Tokyo District Court enforced the California judgment despite the licensing agreement's violation of the Foreign Exchange and Foreign Trade Control Law.

A party who has a final and conclusive judgment rendered in another country may wish to have the courts of Japan give it effect so that he can execute upon the assets of the defendant located in Japan. To have a judgment given such effect it must satisfy the following conditions:

(1) That the jurisdiction of the foreign court is not denied in laws and orders or treaty;
(2) That the defendant defeated, being a Japanese, has received service of summons or any other necessary orders to commence procedure otherwise by a public notice or has appeared without receiving service thereof;
(3) That the judgment of a foreign court is not contrary to the public order or good morals in Japan;
(4) That there is mutual guarantee.[40]

For an American wishing to have a final and conclusive judgment of an American court given effect in Japan, the only two conditions that might possibly prove troublesome are (3) and (4). As far as I can tell, however, in no nonfamily law matter so far has a Japanese court ever denied recognition to a foreign judgment on the ground that the foreign court's judgment violates the public policy of Japan. One writer has even gone so far as to state the following: "Some scholars even claim that a foreign judgment must be enforced if its Decree ... is not against public policy on its face: a Japanese court is not allowed to look behind the face of the decree and inquire into the nature of the underlying transaction of the original claim even in dealing with the issue of public order and good morals. It follows then that any foreign money judgment must be enforced in Japan, be it based on gamblings or other immoral transactions [footnotes omitted]."[41]

The requirement of a reciprocal guarantee is potentially a much more difficult issue for the American seeking to enforce a judgment in Japan. Americans, though, need not worry. Since 1933 it seems well settled in Japan that American judgments satisfy the reciprocity requirement. In that year, the Japanese Supreme Court (then called the Great Court of Cassation) declared:

The requirement of mutual guarantee under the CCP Article 200 (iv) is met where the particular country, in accordance with a treaty or domestic law, grants full effect to a Japanese judgment, without reexamination of the merits, with such requirements as are similar to or more generous than those provided for in the CCP Article 200. The decision below examined the case law of several states in the United States, and found, relying on the Exhibit A No. 4 that there was mutual guarantee in the above meaning. When we look into the Exhibit, it is not unreasonable or impossible to find so. There may be such circumstances in California as the appellants contend [concerning political and economical discrimination against Japanese people]. Again, there may be such rules of law in the United States as the appellants allege [concerning jurisdiction based on transient presence and special appearance]. But such facts do not affect the conclusion that there is mutual guarantee in the above meaning. Accordingly, the appellant's contentions are all groundless.[42]

Since then, Japanese courts have on several occasions emphatically reaffirmed that American judgments satisfy the Japanese requirement of reciprocity; in fact, a number of American judgments have been enforced by Japanese courts since then.[43]

If an American or an American corporation wants to serve process on a Japanese corporation or citizen in Japan, the governing treaty is the 1964 Convention on the Service Abroad of Judicial and Extrajudicial Documents in Civil or Commercial Matters (a copy is affixed as Appendix C to this chapter). The 1964 Convention states that if service is attempted to be sent by certified mail, return receipt requested, that is not an effective service of process. Although Article 10(a) of the Convention provides that one does have "the freedom to send judicial documents, by postal channels, directly to persons abroad," it does not treat this act as effective service of judicial documents.[44] Sending service and effecting it are two totally different matters under the 1964 Convention.

To make an effective service of process by sending a judicial document to a Japanese citizen or corporation in Japan, the original document and a Japanese translation of it should be sent through diplomatic channels to the Japanese Ministry of Foreign Affairs in Tokyo (in Japanese, the "Gaimusho"). The Ministry of Foreign Affairs will transfer the document to the Japanese Supreme Court which will then transmit it to the proper district court which has jurisdiction over the Japanese defendant. All of the proceedings are done without cost to the American party. The American in effecting this service of process must guard against several common errors:

(1) although Article 10(b) and (c) of the Convention authorize service of judicial documents directly to officials or other competent persons of the state of destination, this course of action should not be taken in the case of Japan. It is not possible in Japan to obtain service of process in a lawsuit filed in the United States directly through Japanese officials or other persons in Japan without going through diplomatic channels. Japan has set up the Foreign Ministry as the sole method of service of process;[45]

(2) the original document must be accompanied by a Japanese translation. If it is not, the Japanese will still transmit it. If the defendant refuses to accept it, however, and no translation accompanies it, effective service of process has not occurred;[46]

(3) service of process by certified mail, return receipt requested,

directly on a Japanese defendant as was discussed, does not satisfy the dictates of Article 200 of the Japanese Code of Civil Procedure.[47]

If an American decides to institute suit in Japan, there are several major differences between litigation in the United States and in Japan of which he should be aware. The topic of litigation in Japan is obviously a complex and extensive one. I will be brief in my discussion of litigation in Japan and try merely to discuss the major points. For a more complete discussion, I suggest the reader consult such works as Hideo Tanaka's *The Japanese Legal System*,[48] *Law & the Legal Process in Japan*[49] by Professors Henderson and Haley, and Professor Noda's *Introduction to Japanese Law*.[50]

One major difference between litigation in the two countries is that when one files suit in Japan a fixed amount of revenue stamps must be purchased. The Japanese believe that forcing the plaintiff to purchase revenue stamps prevents abuse of suit. In 1981, for example, a plaintiff in Japan asking for ¥100 million in damages (about $400,000) had to buy ¥600,000 in revenue stamps (about $2,400). The plaintiff in litigation brought in Japan also must buy a certain amount of revenue stamps to cover service of process by the court; the amount usually to be bought is ¥5,000.[51] Not only must the plaintiff in Japan buy these revenue stamps, but if he does not have a domicile, office, or business in Japan, he must in addition offer security to the court for the court costs if the defendant so moves.[52]

Pretrial procedure is a very different matter in Japan than it is in the United States. There is no discovery process, no sending of interrogatories to the other side, and no depositions taken of witnesses. Instead, in the normal case after the complaint is filed, the case is assigned to a particular judicial bench, and a judge or three-judge panel assigns to the case a first trial date. Usually, there is about a one- to two-month period between the complaint's filing date and the first trial date to allow the defendant to prepare his defense.[53]

Trials in Japan are very different from those in the United States. Japan has no jury trials today, to cite one major difference.[54] Rarely are Japanese trials or hearings held consecutively. After the first day of a trial, the date assigned for the case is not the next day but rather a date usually one month or a month and a half later; similarly, after the second day of a trial, the next date assigned is usually about a month later. The court hearings continue in this protracted way until a judgment is rendered.[55] In addition, unlike the practice in the United States, frequently in Japan it is the judge who will direct which witnesses are to be called and the questions to be put to them.[56]

One reason for the protracted trial schedule in Japan is the emphasis in that nation on settlement. During the intervals between court dates, the parties encounter strong societal pressure to settle their dispute.[57]

One famous observer of the emphasis on settlement in the Japanese system has written that "[a]t his discretion the judge can try to compromise the lawsuit at any stage of the proceeding; and since the trial proceeds by a series of intermittent hearings from the time of filing until judgment, the case is continuously at trial. The judge can therefore use his considerable influence at any time to obtain a settlement [citation omitted]."[58]

Even the procedure as to appeals is different in Japan as compared with that in the United States. In Japan, the parties in the first civil appellate proceeding (called kōso) have much more freedom than parties in the United States do to introduce new evidence.[59] The second appeal in Japan, jōkoku,[60] is much more freely allowed than are appeals to the United States Supreme Court or to state supreme courts: the grounds of appeal in Japan are wider, and there is no procedure comparable to the American writ of certiorari.[61]

A topic of obvious interest to Americans doing business in Japan is that of secured transactions. The Japanese laws in this area are similar to those of the United States before the adoption of the Uniform Commercial Code.[62] The Japanese laws today rest upon a foundation of various security devices imported by Japan in the late nineteenth century based on French and German models to which have been added newer forms developed by legislation and custom to meet the needs of her economy. Probably the most important security device in Japan is the pledge. Other important ones are the hypothec, enterprise security, assignment as security, retention of title, and use of a trust.

The classical form of security interest available for movables in Japan is the pledge. "Movable property" under Japanese law encompasses physical items which are movable and bearer obligations.[63] Pledge rights are usually created by a contract in which the pledgor delivers the particular collateral to the pledgee with the intent that it will be security for an obligation which may be his own or that of a third party.[64] The collateral must satisfy the following criteria: it must be in existence, identifiable, and assignable.[65] Delivery does not have to be actual; the pledgor can direct a third party who has custody of the collateral to hold it now for the pledgee.

Any obligation can be secured by a pledge. Unless, though, the pledgee is deprived of the collateral by an illegal act such as a theft, he retains his pledge rights only as long as he or his agent has the collateral. If he does not have the collateral, he has no pledge rights to assert against the holder of the collateral.[66]

The pledgee does have some duties in regard to the collateral. As one might expect, he must preserve the collateral in good condition and return it to the pledgor when the underlying obligation is satisfied.[67] In the usual case he cannot without the pledgor's consent use the collateral, lease it, or himself give it as security.[68]

If the collateral is based on a money debt and the debtor defaults, the pledgee can receive preferential satisfaction of his claim from the collateral. In addition, as a creditor the pledgee can proceed against the debtor's general assets as well. If the debtor defaults and the collateral pledged is a collateral instrument, the pledgee can simply wait for the obligation to be performed.[69] If the proceeds are money, he can apply them to the debt.[70] If they are not, the pledge covers them as well, and he can enforce his rights against them.[71]

Another type of secured interest in Japan is the hypothec, the civil law system counterpart to the common law's statutory mortgage. According to the Japanese Civil Code, the hypothec is a security device only for immovable property.[72] Hypothecation rights come into existence through an agreement by which a hypothetec is established without the transfer of possession.[73] Normally, a hypothec is perfected by recording or registration.[74]

Another area of obvious importance to the American doing business in Japan is that of the rights of creditors under Japanese law. Probably the most dramatic difference between U.S. and Japanese law in this field is that in Japan there are no secured creditors; all creditors are treated alike. The creditor under Japanese law who attached the defendant's property does not obtain a priority or lien superior to non-attaching creditors. All creditors have equal rights to such property.[75]

Another major difference in the rights of creditors is that in Japan there is no "due process" requirement as there is under American law for an attachment or provisional injunction.[76] With some exceptions, all attachments and injunctions in Japan can be obtained in a hearing based upon evidence presented by the creditor with no requirement of notice to the debtor.[77] If a creditor does wish to attach the debtor's property or obtain an injunction against him, the creditor must put up a cash bond as security.[78] There is apparently no statutory rule as to how much the bond must be, but it usually seems to be set at the greater amount of one-third the value of the creditor's claim or one-third the value of the debtor's asset.[79] Unlike the case in the United States, there are no bondsmen in Japan; in the usual case the creditor must thus raise the cash bond himself.

NOTES

1. Horei, Art. 7(1).
2. *Id.*, Art. 7(2).
3. *Id.*, Art. 9(2).
4. Code of Civil Procedure, Art. 25, in II EHS LA 7. It should be noted that EHS (Eibun-Horei-Sha) puts out a *Law Bulletin Series* of the major Japanese statutes. The American lawyer planning to concentrate on helping American clients enter the Japanese market would profit by subscribing to this series.

5. *Appeal of Japan Domestic Airline*, 16 Kaminshu 1154 (Osaka High Ct., June 27, 1965).

6. *Tokyo Marine and Fire Ins. K.K. v. Royal Interocean Lines*, 14 Kaminshu 1477 (Kobe Dist. Ct., July 18, 1963). The holding in that case was later affirmed by the Japanese Supreme Court. 29 Minshu 1554 (S. Ct., November 28, 1975), *aff'g* Hanrei Jiho (No. 586) 29 (Osaka High Ct., December 15, 1969).

7. Horei, Art. 3(1).

8. *Id.*, Art. 3(2).

9. *Id.*, Art. 4(1).

10. For the standard of legal incompetency under Japanese law, *see* Japanese Civil Code, Art. 7.

11. Horei, Art. 4(2).

12. *Id.*, Art. 3.

13. Commercial Code, Art. 479, in II EHS JA 127.

14. *Id.*, Art. 481.

15. In one case, for example, an action on a promissory note brought by a foreign corporation was dismissed by the Japanese courts because the foreign corporation had not satisfied the registration requirement. *Gustaf Foch Gmbh. v. Maruzen K.K.*, 22 Minshu 811 (Gr. Ct. Cass., August 24, 1943).

16. Commercial Code, Art. 498, in II EHS JA 133.

17. *See infra* text accompanying note 13 in Chapter 2.

18. Code of Civil Procedure, Art. 1, in II EHS LA 4.

19. *Id.*, Art. 8, in II EHS LA 5.

20. *Id.*, Art. 15, in II EHS LA 6.

21. *Id.*, Art. 12, in II EHS LA 5.

22. *Id.*, Art. 8, in II EHS LA 5.

23. R. Schlesinger, *Comparative Law* 293 (3rd ed. 1970).

24. *Id.*, 293 n.87a. The U.S. rule today is quite different. *See, e.g., Shaffer v. Heitner*, 433 U.S. 186 (1977).

25. *See, e.g.*, Fujita, "Procedural Fairness to Foreign Litigants as Stressed by Japanese Courts," 12 *Int'l Lawyer* 795, 799 (1978).

26. 10 Kaminshu 1204 (Tokyo Dist. Ct., June 11, 1959).

27. *Id.*, at 1213.

28. Code of Civil Procedure, Art. 5, in II EHS LA 5.

29. *X v. Y*, Hanrei Times (No. 251) 301 (Tokyo Dist. Ct., March 27, 1970).

30. Article 1247 of the French Civil Code states as follows:

Payment must be made at the place designated in the agreement. If payment is to be made of a definite and specified thing, and a place is not designated, payment must be made at the place where the thing was located when the obligation was contracted.

Support which is legally due must be paid at the domicile or residence of the person who is to receive it, unless the court orders otherwise.

In all other cases, payment must be made at the obligee's domicile.

Ordinance No. 58-1298 of December 23, 1958. *See*, A. von Mehren and J. Gordley, *The Civil Law System* 1175 (2nd ed. 1977).

31. JETRO (Japanese External Trade Organization) has stated that the usual practice in disputes involving Japanese "is to resort first to discussions

between the parties involved or to introduce a third party arbitrator." *See,* JETRO, *Contracts and International Trade,* JETRO Business Information Service 6, 2 (1978).

32. Fujita, *supra* note 25, at 801.

33. The JCAA was set up under the Japan Chamber of Commerce, principally upon the initiative of the Federation of Economic Organizations, the Japan Trade Association, and the Japan Federation of Banking Associations. *See* JETRO, *Contracts and International Trade,* JETRO Business Information Service 6, 4 (1978).

34. *See, e.g.,* Fujita, *supra* note 25, at 801-802.

35. *Compania de Transportes del Mar S.A. v. Mataichi K.K.,* 4 Kaminshu 502 (Tokyo Dist. Ct., April 10, 1953).

36. *See, e.g., American President Lines v. Soubra K.K.,* 10 Kaminshu 2232 (Tokyo Dist. Ct., January 25, 1958).

37. Fujita, *supra* note 25, at 808.

38. 3 Int'l Trans. Case Rptr. (Doi's ed.) 583 (Tokyo Dist. Ct., May 28, 1970) as cited in Fujita, *supra* note 25, at 809 n.56.

39. Fujita, *supra* note 25, at 808.

40. Code of Civil Procedure, Art. 200, in II EHS LA 41.

41. Fujita, *supra* note 25, at 806.

42. *Z. Witosky and Co.,* Shimbun (No. 3670) 16, 17 (Gr. Ct. Cass., December 5, 1933).

43. *See, e.g., P.F. Collier, Inc. v. Gate,* Hanrei Jiho (No. 625) 66 (Tokyo Dist. Ct., October 24, 1970); *Western Hardwood Lumber Co. v. W.J. Harman and Co.,* 8 Kaminshu 525 (Tokyo Dist. Ct., March 19, 1957).

44. One Japanese attorney has been quoted as saying that he "advised a Japanese client to completely ignore procedures that took place in Houston, Texas, where service had been sent by certified mail, return receipt requested." "Question and Answer Session," in *Current Legal Aspects of Doing Business in Japan and East Asia* 239, 241 (J. Haley ed. 1978).

45. The Convention states that service of process can be effected through officials or other competent persons as long as "the State of destination does not object." Convention on the Service Abroad of Judicial and Extrajudicial Documents in Civil or Commercial Matters, October 28, 1964, Art. 10. Japan, though, has objected to this provision. *See, e.g.,* "Question and Answer Session," *supra* note 44, at 241.

46. Tasuku Matsuo, "Dispute Resolution in Japan," in *Legal Aspects of Doing Business with Japan* 173, 174 (I. Shapiro chmn. 1981).

47. *See infra* text accompanying note 44.

48. Published in 1976.

49. Published in 1978.

50. Published in 1976.

51. *See, e.g.,* Matsuo, *supra* note 46, at 175.

52. Code of Civil Procedure, Art. 107, in II EHS LA 23.

53. *See, e.g.,* Matsuo, *supra* note 46, at 181.

54. *See infra* footnote 35 in Chapter 2.

55. *See, e.g., The Japanese Legal System* 475 (H. Tanaka ed. 1976).

56. This practice, though, was much more common in the system that existed

until the end of World War II and followed the example of German civil law. Since then, American practices have strongly influenced Japanese courtroom procedure. *See, e.g.*, Kohji Tanable, "The Process of Litigation: An Experiment with the Adversary System," in *Law in Japan-The Legal Order in a Changing Society* 73-110 (A. von Mehren ed. 1963).

57. For an excellent discussion of the societal push in Japan to settlement, *see* D. Henderson, *Conciliation and Japanese Law* (1965).

58. *Id.*, at volume II page 250. This pressure on settlement is reflected by the Code of Civil Procedure which states:

The court may, whatever stage the suit may be in, attempt to carry out compromise or have a commissioned judge or an entrusted judge try the same.

2. The court, a commissioned judge or an entrusted judge may for compromise order the principal party or his legal representative to appear before court.

Code of Civil Procedure, Art. 136, II EHS LA 28.

59. For more information on kōso proceedings, *see infra* text accompanying note 41 in Chapter 2.

60. For more information on jōkoku appeals, *see infra* text accompanying note 42 in Chapter 2.

61. A large number, however, of the jōkoku appeals brought before the Supreme Court of Japan are dismissed in a brief opinion which simply states that the appellant has not presented any ground for appellate review. *See, e.g.*, Tanaka, *supra* note 55, at 475-476.

62. Coleman, "The Japanese and Korean Law of Secured Transactions," 2 *Hastings Int'l and Comp. L. R.* 21 (1979). This article is an excellent and detailed discussion of this topic.

63. Civil Code, Arts. 85, 86(2), 86(3), in II EHS FA 16.

64. *Id.*, Art. 342, in II EHS FA 56-57.

65. *Id.*, Art. 343, in II FA 57.

66. *Id.*, Art. 352, in II FA 58.

67. *Id.*, Art. 298, in II FA 49.

68. *Id.*, Art. 298(2), in II FA 49.

69. *Id.*, Art. 367, in II FA 59.

70. *Id.*, Art. 367(2), in II FA 59.

71. *Id.*, Art. 367 (4), in I FA 60.

72. The Japanese Commercial Code does provide for the hypothecation of some movables. Coleman, *supra* note 62, at 28.

73. Civil Code, Art. 369, in II FA 60.

74. *Id.*, Art. 373, in II FA 60-61.

75. This rule has been vehemently criticized by Japanese scholars as being overly protective of the "lazy" creditor. *See, e.g.*, Mikazuki Arika, "Hozen shobun no tuikei" ("Structure of Provisional Disposition"), in *Horitsu Bunkasha* 477 (1966).

76. *See, e.g., Sniadach v. Family Finance Corp.*, 395 U.S. 335 (1969).

77. Code of Civil Procedure, Arts. 737, 740, 741 in II LA 147, 148.

78. *Id.*, Art. 741, in II LA 148.

79. *See, e.g.,* Tasuku Matsuo and Richard Vliet, "Creditor's Rights under Japanese Law," in *Current Legal Aspects of Doing Business in Japan and East Asia* 202, 207 (J. Haley ed. 1978).

Countries and Regions Having Arbitration Agreements with Japan

Argentina
Australia
Austria
Belgium
Botswana
Bulgaria
Burma
Central African Empire
Chile
Cuba
Czechoslovakia
Dahomey
Democratic Kampuchea
Denmark
East Germany
Ecuador
El Salvador
Federation of Arab
  Republics
Finland
France
F.R. Germany

Ghana
Greece
Hong Kong
Hungary
India
Ireland
Israel
Italy
Luxembourg
Malagasy Republic
Malta
Mauritius
Mexico
Morocco
New Zealand
Nigeria
Norway
Pakistan
People's Republic of
  China
Peru
Poland

Portugal
Romania
South Korea
Spain
Sri Lanka
Sweden
Switzerland
Syria
Tanzania
Thailand
The Netherlands
The Philippines
Trinidad and Tobago
Tunisia
U.K.
Ukraine
U.S.A.
U.S.S.R.
Vatican City
White Russia
Yugoslavia

Convention on the Recognition and Enforcement of Foreign Arbitral Awards of 1958 (New York Convention)

Reproduced From Register of Texts of Conventions and Other Instruments Concerning International Trade Law, Volume II, United Nations 1973.

Article I

1. This Convention shall apply to the recognition and enforcement of arbitral awards made in the territory of a State other than the State where the recognition and enforcement of such awards are sought, and arising out of differences between persons, whether

---

[1] The Convention entered into force on 7 June 1959.

The following States have deposited their ratifications (r) or accessions (a) with the Secretary-General of the United Nations:

Austria	(a) —	2 May	1961
Botswana	(a) —	20 December	1971
Bulgaria	(r) —	10 October	1961
Byelorussian SSR	(r) —	15 November	1960
Central African Republic	(a) —	15 October	1962
Ceylon	(r) —	9 April	1962
Czechoslovakia	(r) —	10 July	1959
Ecuador	(r) —	3 January	1962
Egypt	(a) —	9 March	1959
Federal Republic of Germany	(r) —	30 June	1961
Finland	(r) —	19 January	1962
France	(r) —	26 June	1959
Ghana	(a) —	9 April	1968
Greece	(a) —	16 July	1962
Hungary	(a) —	5 March	1962
India	(r) —	13 July	1960
Israel	(r) —	5 January	1959
Italy	(a) —	31 January	1969
Japan	(a) —	20 June	1961
Khmer Republic	(a) —	5 January	1960
Madagascar	(a) —	16 July	1962
Mexico	(a) —	14 April	1971
Morocco	(a) —	12 February	1959
Netherlands	(r) —	24 April	1964
Niger	(a) —	14 October	1964
Nigeria	(a) —	17 March	1970
Norway	(a) —	14 March	1961
Philippines	(r) —	6 July	1967
Poland	(r) —	3 October	1961
Romania	(a) —	13 September	1961
Sweden	(r) —	20 January	1972
Switzerland	(r) —	1 June	1965
Syrian Arab Republic	(a) —	9 March	1959
Thailand	(a) —	21 December	1959
Trinidad and Tobago	(a) —	14 February	1966
Tunisia	(a) —	17 July	1967
Ukrainian SSR	(r) —	10 October	1960

(Continued on next page.)

physical or legal. It shall also apply to arbitral awards not considered as domestic award in the State where their recognition and enforcement are sought.

2. The term " arbitral awards " shall include not only awards made by arbitrator appointed for each case but also those made by permanent arbitral bodies to which the parties have submitted.

3. When signing, ratifying or acceding to this Convention, or notifying extension under article X hereof, any State may on the basis of reciprocity declare that it will apply the Convention to the recognition and enforcement of awards made only in the territory of another Contracting State. It may also declare that it will apply the Convention only to differences arising out of legal relationships, whether contractual or not, which are considered as commercial under the national law of the State making such declaration

Article II

1. Each Contracting State shall recognize an agreement in writing under which the parties undertake to submit to arbitration all or any differences which have arisen or which may arise between them in respect of a defined legal relationship, whether contractual or not, concerning a subject matter capable of settlement by arbitration.

2. The term " agreement in writing " shall include an arbitral clause in a contract or an arbitration agreement, signed by the parties or contained in an exchange of letters or telegrams.

3. The court of a Contracting State, when seized of an action in a matter in respect of which the parties have made an agreement within the meaning of this article, at the request of one of the parties, refer the parties to arbitration, unless it finds that the said agreement is null and void, inoperative or incapable of being performed.

Article III

Each Contracting State shall recognize arbitral awards as binding and enforce them in accordance with the rules of procedure of the territory where the award is relied upon, under the conditions laid down in the following articles. There shall not be imposed substantially more onerous conditions or higher fees or charges on the recognition or enforcement of arbitral awards to which this Convention applies than are imposed on the recognition or enforcement of domestic arbitral awards.

Article IV

1. To obtain the recognition and enforcement mentioned in the preceding article, the party applying for recognition and enforcement shall, at the time of the application, supply:

(a) The duly authenticated original award or a duly certified copy thereof;

(b) The original agreement referred to in article II or a duly certified copy thereof.

2. If the said award or agreement is not made in an official language of the country in which the award is relied upon, the party applying for recognition and enforcement of the award shall produce a translation of these documents into such

---

(Cont.)   Union of Soviet Socialist Republics   (r) — 24 August   1960
          United Republic of Tanzania   (a) — 13 October   1964
          United States of America   (a) — 30 September 1970
    The following States have signed the Convention: Argentina, Belgium, Costa Rica, El Salvador, Jordan, Luxembourg, Monaco, Pakistan.

anguage. The translation snall be certified by an official or sworn translator or by a diplomatic or consular agent.

Article V

1. Recognition and enforcement of the award may be refused, at the request of the party against whom it is invoked, only if that party furnishes to the competent authority where the recognition and enforcement is sought, proof that:

(a) The parties to the agreement referred to in article II were, under the law applicable to them, under some incapacity, or the said agreement is not valid under the law to which the parties have subjected it or, failing any indication thereon, under the law of the country where the award was made; or

(b) The party against whom the award is invoked was not given proper notice of the appointment of the arbitrator or of the arbitration proceedings or was otherwise unable to present his case; or

(c) The award deals with a difference not contemplated by or not falling within the terms of the submission to arbitration, or it contains decisions on matters beyond the scope of the submission to arbitration, provided that, if the decisions on matters submitted to arbitration can be separated from those not so submitted, that part of the award which contains decisions on matters submitted to arbitration may be recognized and enforced; or

(d) The composition of the arbitral authority or the arbitral procedure was not in accordance with the agreement of the parties, or, failing such agreement, was not in accordance with the law of the country where the arbitration took place; or

(e) The award has not yet become binding on the parties, or has been set aside or suspended by a competent authority of the country in which, or under the law of which, that award was made.

2. Recognition and enforcement of an arbitral award may also be refused if the competent authority in the country where recognition and enforcement is sought finds that:

(a) The subject matter of the difference is not capable of settlement by arbitration under the law of that country; or

(b) The recognition or enforcement of the award would be contrary to the public policy of that country.

Article VI

If an application for the setting aside or suspension of the award has been made to a competent authority referred to in article V (1) (e), the authority before which the award is sought to be relied upon may, if it considers it proper, adjourn the decision on the enforcement of the award and may also, on the application of the party claiming enforcement of the award, order the other party to give suitable security.

Article VII

1. The provisions of the present Convention shall not affect the validity of multilateral or bilateral agreements concerning the recognition and enforcement of arbitral awards entered into by the Contracting States nor deprive any interested party of any right he may have to avail himself of an arbitral award in the manner and to the extent allowed by the law or the treaties of the country where such award is sought to be relied upon.

2. The Geneva Protocol on Arbitration Clauses of 1923 and the Geneva Convention on the Execution of Foreign Arbitral Awards of 1927 shall cease to have effect between

Contracting States on their becoming bound and to the extent that they become bound by this Convention.

Article VIII

1. This Convention shall be open until 31 December 1958 for signature on behal of any Member of the United Nations and also on behalf of any other State which is o hereafter becomes a member of any specialized agency of the United Nations, or whic is or hereafter becomes a party to the Statute of the International Court of Justice, or an other State to which an invitation has been addressed by the General Assembly of th United Nations.

2. This Convention shall be ratified and the instrument of ratification shall b deposited with the Secretary-General of the United Nations.

Article IX

1. This Convention shall be open for accession to all States referred to i article VIII.

2. Accession shall be effected by the deposit of an instrument of accession with th Secretary-General of the United Nations.

Article X

1. Any State may, at the time of signature, ratification or accession, declare tha this Convention shall extend to all or any of the territories for the international relation of which it is responsible. Such a declaration shall take effect when the Convention enter into force for the State concerned.

2. At any time thereafter any such extension shall be made by notification addresse to the Secretary-General of the United Nations and shall take effect as from the nine tieth day after the day of receipt by the Secretary-General of the United Nations of th notification, or as from the date of entry into force of the Convention for the Stat concerned, whichever is the later.

3. With respect to those territories to which this Convention is not extended at th time of signature, ratification or accession, each State concerned shall consider th possibility of taking the necessary steps in order to extend the application of this Conventio to such territories, subject, where necessary for constitutional reasons, to the consent c the Governments of such territories.

Article XI

In the case of a federal or non-unitary State, the following provisions shall apply

(a) With respect to those articles of this Convention that come within th legislative jurisdiction of the federal authority, the obligations of the federal Governmer shall to this extent be the same as those of Contracting States which are not federa States;

(b) With respect to those articles of this Convention that come within th legislative jurisdiction of constituent states or provinces which are not, under th constitutional system of the federation, bound to take legislative action, the federa Government shall bring such articles with a favourable recommendation to the notic of the appropriate authorities of constituent states or provinces at the earliest possibl moment;

(c) A federal State Party to this Convention shall, at the request of any other Contracting State transmitted through the Secretary-General of the United Nations, supply a statement of the law and practice of the federation and its constituent units in regard to any particular provision of this Convention, showing the extent to which effect has been given to that provision by legislative or other action.

Article XII

1. This Convention shall come into force on the ninetieth day following the date of deposit of the third instrument of ratification or accession.

2. For each State ratifying or acceding to this Convention after the deposit of the third instrument of ratification or accession, this Convention shall enter into force on the ninetieth day after deposit by such State of its instrument of ratification or accession.

Article XIII

1. Any Contracting State may denounce this Convention by a written notification to the Secretary-General of the United Nations. Denunciation shall take effect one year after the date of receipt of the notification by the Secretary-General.

2. Any State which has made a declaration or notification under article X may, at any time thereafter, by notification to the Secretary-General of the United Nations, declare that this Convention shall cease to extend to the territory concerned one year after the date of the receipt of the notification by the Secretary-General.

3. This Convention shall continue to be applicable to arbitral awards in respect of which recognition or enforcement proceedings have been instituted before the denunciation takes effect.

Article XIV

A Contracting State shall not be entitled to avail itself of the present Convention against other Contracting States except to the extent that it is itself bound to apply the Convention.

Article XV

The Secretary-General of the United Nations shall notify the States contemplated in article VIII of the following:

(a) Signatures and ratifications in accordance with article VIII;

(b) Accessions in accordance with article IX;

(c) Declarations and notifications under articles I, X and XI;

(d) The date upon which this Convention enters into force in accordance with article XII;

(e) Denunciations and notifications in accordance with article XIII.

Article XVI

1. This Convention, of which the Chinese, English, French, Russian and Spanish texts shall be equally authentic, shall be deposited in the archives of the United Nations.

2. The Secretary-General of the United Nations shall transmit a certified copy of this Convention to the States contemplated in article VIII.

Convention on the Service Abroad of Judicial and Extra-Judicial Documents in Civil or Commercial Matters

APPENDIX C

Les Etats signataires de la présente Convention,

Désirant créer les moyens appropriés pour que les actes judiciaires et extrajudiciaires qui doivent être signifiés ou notifiés à l'étranger soient connus de leurs destinataires en temps utile,

Soucieux d'améliorer à cette fin l'entraide judiciaire mutuelle en simplifiant et en accélérant la procédure,

Ont résolu de conclure une Convention à ces effets et sont convenus des dispositions suivantes:

ARTICLE PREMIER

La présente Convention est applicable, en matière civile ou commerciale, dans tous les cas où un acte judiciaire ou extrajudiciaire doit être transmis à l'étranger pour y être signifié ou notifié.

La Convention ne s'applique pas lorsque l'adresse du destinataire de l'acte n'est pas connue.

CHAPITRE I – ACTES JUDICIAIRES

ARTICLE 2

Chaque Etat contractant désigne une Autorité centrale qui assume, conformément aux articles 3 à 6, la charge de recevoir les demandes de signification ou de notification en provenance d'un autre Etat contractant et d'y donner suite.

The States signatory to the present Convention,

Desiring to create appropriate means to ensure that judicial and extrajudicial documents to be served abroad shall be brought to the notice of the addressee in sufficient time,

Desiring to improve the organisation of mutual judicial assistance for that purpose by simplifying and expediting the procedure,

Have resolved to conclude a Convention to this effect and have agreed upon the following provisions:

ARTICLE 1

The present Convention shall apply in all cases, in civil or commercial matters, where there is occasion to transmit a judicial or extrajudicial document for service abroad.

This Convention shall not apply where the address of the person to be served with the document is not known.

CHAPTER I – JUDICIAL DOCUMENTS

ARTICLE 2

Each contracting State shall designate a Central Authority which will undertake to receive requests for service coming from other contracting States and to proceed in conformity with the provisions of articles 3 to 6.

---

[1] Texte complet de l'Acte final, voir *Actes et Documents de la Dixième session (1964)*, tome I.

L'Autorité centrale est organisée selon les modalités prévues par l'Etat requis.

Each State shall organise the Centra Authority in conformity with its own law.

ARTICLE 3

L'autorité ou l'officier ministériel compétents selon les lois de l'Etat d'origine adresse à l'Autorité centrale de l'Etat requis une demande conforme à la formule modèle annexée à la présente Convention, sans qu'il soit besoin de la légalisation des pièces ni d'une autre formalité équivalente.

La demande doit être accompagnée de l'acte judiciaire ou de sa copie, le tout en double exemplaire.

ARTICLE 3

The authority or judicial officer competent under the law of the State in which the documents originate shall forward to the Central Authority of the State addressed a request conforming to the model annexed to the present Convention, without any requirement of legalisation or other equivalent formality.

The document to be served or a copy thereof shall be annexed to the request. The request and the document shall both eb furnished in duplicate.

ARTICLE 4

Si l'Autorité centrale estime que les dispositions de la Convention n'ont pas été respectées, elle en informe immédiatement le requérant en précisant les griefs articulés à l'encontre de la demande.

ARTICLE 4

If the Central Authority considers that the request does not comply with the provisions of the present Convention it shall promptly inform the applicant and specify its objections to the request.

ARTICLE 5

L'Autorité centrale de l'Etat requis procède ou fait procéder à la signification ou à la notification de l'acte :

a) soit selon les formes prescrites par la législation de l'Etat requis pour la signification ou la notification des actes dressés dans ce pays et qui sont destinés aux personnes se trouvant sur son territoire;

b) soit selon la forme particulière demandée par le requérant, pourvu que celle-ci ne soit pas incompatible avec la loi de l'Etat requis.

Sauf le cas prévu à l'alinéa premier, lettre b), l'acte peut toujours être remis au destinataire qui l'accepte volontairement.

Si l'acte doit être signifié ou notifié conformément à l'alinéa premier, l'Autorité centrale peut demander que l'acte soit rédigé ou traduit dans la langue ou une des langues officielles de son pays.

La partie de la demande conforme à la formule modèle annexée à la présente Convention, qui contient les éléments essentiels de l'acte, est remise au destinataire.

ARTICLE 5

The Central Authority of the State addressed shall itself serve the document or shall arrange to have it served by an appropriate agency, either –

(a) by a method prescribed by its internal law for the service of documents in domestic actions upon persons who are within its territory, or

(b) by a particular method requested by the applicant, unless such a method is incompatible with the law of the State addressed.

Subject to sub-paragraph (b) of the first paragraph of this article, the document may always be served by delivery to an addressee who accepts it voluntarily.

If the document is to be served under the first paragraph above, the Central Authority may require the document to be written in, or translated into, the official language or one of the official languages of the State addressed.

That part of the request, in the form attached to the present Convention, which contains a summary of the document to be served, shall be served with the document.

ARTICLE 6

L'Autorité centrale de l'Etat requis ou

ARTICLE 6

The Central Authority of the State ad-

toute autorité qu'il aura désignée à cette fin établit une attestation conforme à la formule modèle annexée à la présente Convention.

L'attestation relate l'exécution de la demande; elle indique la forme, le lieu et la date de l'exécution ainsi que la personne à laquelle l'acte a été remis. Le cas échéant, elle précise le fait qui aurait empêché l'exécution.

Le requérant peut demander que l'attestation qui n'est pas établie par l'Autorité centrale ou par une autorité judiciaire soit visée par l'une de ces autorités.

L'attestation est directement adressée au requérant.

dressed or any authority which it may have designated for that purpose, shall complete a certificate in the form of the model annexed to the present Convention.

The certificate shall state that the document has been served and shall include the method, the place and the date of service and the person to whom the document was delivered. If the document has not been served, the certificate shall set out the reasons which have prevented service.

The applicant may require that a certificate not completed by a Central Authority or by a judicial authority shall be countersigned by one of these authorities.

The certificate shall be forwarded directly to the applicant.

ARTICLE 7

Les mentions imprimées dans la formule modèle annexée à la présente Convention sont obligatoirement rédigées soit en langue française, soit en langue anglaise. Elles peuvent, en outre, être rédigées dans la langue ou une des langues officielles de l'Etat d'origine.

Les blancs correspondant à ces mentions sont remplis soit dans la langue de l'Etat requis, soit en langue française, soit en langue anglaise.

ARTICLE 7

The standard terms in the model annexed to the present Convention shall in all cases be written either in French or in English. They may also be written in the official language, or in one of the official languages, of the State in which the documents originate.

The corresponding blanks shall be completed either in the language of the State addressed or in French or in English.

ARTICLE 8

Chaque Etat contractant a la faculté de faire procéder directement, sans contrainte, par les soins de ses agents diplomatiques ou consulaires, aux significations ou notifications d'actes judiciaires aux personnes se trouvant à l'étranger.

Tout Etat peut déclarer s'opposer à l'usage de cette faculté sur son territoire, sauf si l'acte doit être signifié ou notifié à un ressortissant de l'Etat d'origine.

ARTICLE 8

Each contracting State shall be free to effect service of judicial documents upon persons abroad, without application of any compulsion, directly through its diplomatic or consular agents.

Any State may declare that it is opposed to such service within its territory, unless the document is to be served upon a national of the State in which the documents originate.

ARTICLE 9

Chaque Etat contractant a, de plus, la faculté d'utiliser la voie consulaire pour transmettre, aux fins de signification ou de notification, des actes judiciaires aux autorités d'un autre Etat contractant que celui-ci a désignées.

Si des circonstances exceptionnelles l'exigent, chaque Etat contractant a la faculté d'utiliser, aux mêmes fins, la voie diplomatique.

ARTICLE 9

Each contracting State shall be free, in addition, to use consular channels to forward documents, for the purpose of service, to those authorities of another contracting State which are designated by the latter for this purpose.

Each contracting State may, if exceptional circumstances so require, use diplomatic channels for the same purpose.

ARTICLE 10

La présente Convention ne fait pas obstacle, sauf si l'Etat de destination déclare s'y opposer:

a) à la faculté d'adresser directement, par la voie de la poste, des actes judiciaires aux personnes se trouvant à l'étranger,

b) à la faculté, pour les officiers ministériels, fonctionnaires ou autres personnes compétents de l'Etat d'origine, de faire procéder à des significations ou notifications d'actes judiciaires directement par les soins des officiers ministériels, fonctionnaires ou autres personnes compétents de l'Etat de destination,

c) à la faculté, pour toute personne intéressée à une instance judiciaire, de faire procéder à des significations ou notifications d'actes judiciaires directement par les soins des officiers ministériels, fonctionnaires ou autres personnes compétents de l'Etat de destination.

ARTICLE 11

La présente Convention ne s'oppose pas à ce que des Etats contractants s'entendent pour admettre, aux fins de signification ou de notification des actes judiciaires, d'autres voies de transmission que celles prévues par les articles qui précèdent et notamment la communication directe entre leurs autorités respectives.

ARTICLE 12

Les significations ou notifications d'actes judiciaires en provenance d'un Etat contractant ne peuvent donner lieu au paiement ou au remboursement de taxes ou de frais pour les services de l'Etat requis.

Le requérant est tenu de payer ou de rembourser les frais occasionnés par:

a) l'intervention d'un officier ministériel ou d'une personne compétente selon la loi de l'Etat de destination,

b) l'emploi d'une forme particulière.

ARTICLE 13

L'exécution d'une demande de signification ou de notification conforme aux dispositions

ARTICLE 10

Provided the State of destination does not object, the present Convention shall not interfere with –

(a) the freedom to send judicial documents, by postal channels, directly to persons abroad,

(b) the freedom of judicial officers, officials or other competent persons of the State of origin to effect service of judicial documents directly through the judicial officers, officials or other competent persons of the State of destination,

(c) the freedom of any person interested in a judicial proceeding to effect service of judicial documents directly through the judicial officers, officials or other competent persons of the State of destination.

ARTICLE 11

The present Convention shall not prevent two or more contracting States from agreeing to permit, for the purpose of service of judicial documents, channels of transmission other than those provided for in the preceding articles and, in particular, direct communication between their respective authorities.

ARTICLE 12

The service of judicial documents coming from a contracting State shall not give rise to any payment or reimbursement of taxes or costs for the services rendered by the State addressed.

The applicant shall pay or reimburse the costs occasioned by –

(a) the employment of a judicial officer or of a person competent under the law of the State of destination,

(b) the use of a particular method of service.

ARTICLE 13

Where a request for service complies with the terms of the present Convention, the State

de la présente Convention ne peut être refusée que si l'Etat requis juge que cette exécution est de nature à porter atteinte à sa souveraineté ou à sa sécurité.

L'exécution ne peut être refusée pour le seul motif que la loi de l'Etat requis revendique la compétence judiciaire exclusive dans l'affaire en cause ou ne connaît pas de voie de droit répondant à l'objet de la demande.

En cas de refus, l'Autorité centrale en informe immédiatement le requérant et indique les motifs.

Les difficultés qui s'élèveraient à l'occasion de la transmission, aux fins de signification ou de notification, d'actes judiciaires seront réglées par la voie diplomatique.

Lorsqu'un acte introductif d'instance ou un acte équivalent a dû être transmis à l'étranger aux fins de signification ou de notification, selon les dispositions de la présente Convention, et que le défendeur ne comparait pas, le juge est tenu de surseoir à statuer aussi longtemps qu'il n'est pas établi:

a) ou bien que l'acte a été signifié ou notifié selon les formes prescrites par la législation de l'Etat requis pour la signification ou la notification des actes dressés dans ce pays et qui sont destinés aux personnes se trouvant sur son territoire,

b) ou bien que l'acte a été effectivement remis au défendeur ou à sa demeure selon un autre procédé prévu par la présente Convention,

et que, dans chacune de ces éventualités, soit la signification ou la notification, soit la remise a eu lieu en temps utile pour que le défendeur ait pu se défendre.

Chaque Etat contractant a la faculté de déclarer que ses juges, nonobstant les dispositions de l'alinéa premier, peuvent statuer si les conditions suivantes sont réunies, bien qu'aucune attestation constatant soit la signification ou la notification, soit la remise, n'ait été reçue:

a) l'acte a été transmis selon un des modes prévus par la présente Convention,

addressed may refuse to comply therewith only if it deems that compliance would infringe its sovereignty or security.

It may not refuse to comply solely on the ground that, under its internal law, it claims exclusive jurisdiction over the subject-matter of the action or that its internal law would not permit the action upon which the application is based.

The Central Authority shall, in case of refusal, promptly inform the applicant and state the reasons for the refusal.

Difficulties which may arise in connection with the transmission of judicial documents for service shall be settled through diplomatic channels.

Where a writ of summons or an equivalent document had to be transmitted abroad for the purpose of service, under the provisions of the present Convention, and the defendant has not appeared, judgment shall not be given until it is established that –

(a) the document was served by a method prescribed by the internal law of the State addressed for the service of documents in domestic actions upon persons who are within its territory, or

(b) the document was actually delivered to the defendant or to his residence by another method provided for by this Convention,

and that in either of these cases the service or the delivery was effected in sufficient time to enable the defendant to defend.

Each contracting State shall be free to declare that the judge, notwithstanding the provisions of the first paragraph of this article, may give judgment even if no certificate of service or delivery has been received, if all the following conditions are fulfilled –

(a) the document was transmitted by one of the methods provided for in this Convention,

b) un délai que le juge appréciera dans chaque cas particulier et qui sera d'au moins six mois, s'est écoulé depuis la date d'envoi de l'acte,

c) nonobstant toutes diligences utiles auprès des autorités compétentes de l'Etat requis, aucune attestation n'a pu être obtenue.

Le présent article ne fait pas obstacle à ce qu'en cas d'urgence, le juge ordonne toutes mesures provisoires ou conservatoires.

ARTICLE 16

Lorsqu'un acte introductif d'instance ou un acte équivalent a dû être transmis à l'étranger aux fins de signification ou de notification, selon les dispositions de la présente Convention, et qu'une décision a été rendue contre un défendeur qui n'a pas comparu, le juge a la faculté de relever ce défendeur de la forclusion résultant de l'expiration des délais de recours, si les conditions suivantes sont réunies:

a) le défendeur, sans qu'il y ait eu faute de sa part, n'a pas eu connaissance en temps utile dudit acte pour se défendre et de la décision pour exercer un recours,

b) les moyens du défendeur n'apparaissent pas dénués de tout fondement.

La demande tendant au relevé de la forclusion est irrecevable si elle n'est pas formée dans un délai raisonnable à partir du moment où le défendeur a eu connaissance de la décision.

Chaque Etat contractant a la faculté de déclarer que cette demande est irrecevable si elle est formée après l'expiration d'un délai qu'il précisera dans sa déclaration, pourvu que ce délai ne soit pas inférieur à un an à compter du prononcé de la décision.

Le présent article ne s'applique pas aux décisions concernant l'état des personnes.

CHAPITRE II – ACTES EXTRAJUDICIAIRES

ARTICLE 17

Les actes extrajudiciaires émanant des autorités et officiers ministériels d'un Etat contractant peuvent être transmis aux fins de signification ou de notification dans un autre

---

(b) a period of time of not less than six months, considered adequate by the judge in the particular case, has elapsed since the date of the transmission of the document,

(c) no certificate of any kind has been received, even though every reasonable effort has been made to obtain it through the competent authorities of the State addressed.

Notwithstanding the provisions of the preceding paragraphs the judge may order, in case of urgency, any provisional or protective measures.

ARTICLE 16

When a writ of summons or an equivalent document had to be transmitted abroad for the purpose of service, under the provisions of the present Convention, and a judgment has been entered against a defendant who has not appeared, the judge shall have the power to relieve the defendant from the effects of the expiration of the time for appeal from the judgment if the following conditions are fulfilled –

(a) the defendant, without any fault on his part, did not have knowledge of the document in sufficient time to defend, or knowledge of the judgment in sufficient time to appeal, and

(b) the defendant has disclosed a *prima facie* defence to the action on the merits.

An application for relief may be filed only within a reasonable time after the defendant has knowledge of the judgment.

Each contracting State may declare that the application will not be entertained if it is filed after the expiration of a time to be stated in the declaration, but which shall in no case be less than one year following the date of the judgment.

This article shall not apply to judgments concerning status or capacity of persons.

CHAPTER II – EXTRAJUDICIAL DOCUMENTS

ARTICLE 17

Extrajudicial documents emanating from authorities and judicial officers of a contracting State may be transmitted for the purpose of service in another contracting State by the

Etat contractant selon les modes et aux conditions prévus par la présente Convention.

methods and under the provisions of the present Convention.

CHAPITRE III – DISPOSITIONS GÉNÉRALES

CHAPTER III – GENERAL CLAUSES

ARTICLE 18

Tout Etat contractant peut désigner, outre l'Autorité centrale, d'autres autorités dont il détermine les compétences.

Toutefois, le requérant a toujours le droit de s'adresser directement à l'Autorité centrale.

Les Etats fédéraux ont la faculté de désigner plusieurs Autorités centrales.

ARTICLE 18

Each contracting State may designate other authorities in addition to the Central Authority and shall determine the extent of their competence.

The applicant shall, however, in all cases, have the right to address a request directly to the Central Authority.

Federal States shall be free to designate more than one Central Authority.

ARTICLE 19

La présente Convention ne s'oppose pas à ce que la loi interne d'un Etat contractant permette d'autres formes de transmission non prévues dans les articles précédents, aux fins de signification ou de notification, sur son territoire, des actes venant de l'étranger.

ARTICLE 19

To the extent that the internal law of a contracting State permits methods of transmission, other than those provided for in the preceding articles, of documents coming from abroad, for service within its territory, the present Convention shall not affect such provisions.

ARTICLE 20

La présente Convention ne s'oppose pas à ce que des Etats contractants s'entendent pour déroger:

a) à l'article 3, alinéa 2, en ce qui concerne l'exigence du double exemplaire des pièces transmises,

b) à l'article 5, alinéa 3, et à l'article 7, en ce qui concerne l'emploi des langues,

c) à l'article 5, alinéa 4,

d) à l'article 12, alinéa 2.

ARTICLE 20

The present Convention shall not prevent an agreement between any two or more contracting States to dispense with –

(a) the necessity for duplicate copies of transmitted documents as required by the second paragraph of article 3,

(b) the language requirements of the third paragraph of article 5 and article 7,

(c) the provisions of the fourth paragraph of article 5,

(d) the provisions of the second paragraph of article 12.

ARTICLE 21

Chaque Etat contractant notifiera au Ministère des Affaires Etrangères des Pays-Bas soit au moment du dépôt de son instrument de ratification ou d'adhésion, soit ultérieurement:

a) la désignation des autorités prévues aux articles 2 et 18,

b) la désignation de l'autorité compétente pour établir l'attestation prévue à l'article 6,

ARTICLE 21

Each contracting State shall, at the time of the deposit of its instrument of ratification or accession, or at a later date, inform the Ministry of Foreign Affairs of the Netherlands of the following –

(a) the designation of authorities, pursuant to articles 2 and 18,

(b) the designation of the authority competent to complete the certificate pursuant to article 6,

c) la désignation de l'autorité compétente pour recevoir les actes transmis par la voie consulaire selon l'article 9.

Il notifiera, le cas échéant, dans le smêmes conditions:

a) son opposition à l'usage des voies de transmission prévues aux articles 8 et 10,

b) les déclarations prévues aux articles 15, alinéa 2, et 16, alinéa 3,

c) toute modification des désignations, opposition et déclarations mentionnées ci-dessus.

ARTICLE 22

La présente Convention remplacera dans les rapports entre les Etats qui l'auront ratifiée, les articles 1 à 7 des Conventions relatives à la procédure civile, respectivement signées à La Haye, le 17 juillet 1905 et le premier mars 1954, dans la mesure où lesdits Etats sont Parties à l'une ou à l'autre de ces Conventions.

ARTICLE 23

La présente Convention ne porte pas atteinte à l'application de l'article 23 de la Convention relative à la procédure civile, signée à La Haye, le 17 juillet 1905, ni de l'article 24 de celle signée à La Haye, le premier mars 1954.

Ces articles ne sont toutefois applicables que s'il est fait usage de modes de communication identiques à ceux prévus par lesdites Conventions.

ARTICLE 24

Les accords, additionnels auxdites Conventions de 1905 et de 1954, conclus par les Etats contractants, sont considérés comme également applicables à la présente Convention à moins que les Etats intéressés n'en conviennent autrement.

ARTICLE 25

Sans préjudice de l'application des articles 22 et 24, la présente Convention ne déroge pas aux Conventions auxquelles les Etats contractants sont ou seront Parties et qui contiennent

c) the designation of the authority competent to receive documents transmitted by consular channels, pursuant to article 9.

Each contracting State shall similarly inform the Ministry, where appropriate, of –

(a) opposition to the use of methods of transmission pursuant to articles 8 and 10,

(b) declarations pursuant to the second paragraph of article 15 and the third paragraph of article 16,

(c) all modifications of the above designations, oppositions and declarations.

ARTICLE 22

Where Parties to the present Convention are also Parties to one or both of the Conventions on civil procedure signed at The Hague on 17th July 1905, and on 1st March 1954, this Convention shall replace as between them articles 1 to 7 of the earlier Conventions.

ARTICLE 23

The present Convention shall not affect the application of article 23 of the Convention on civil procedure signed at The Hague on 17th July 1905, or of article 24 of the Convention on civil procedure signed at The Hague on 1st March 1954.

These articles shall, however, apply only if methods of communication, identical to those provided for in these Conventions, are used.

ARTICLE 24

Supplementary agreements between Parties to the Conventions of 1905 and 1954 shall be considered as equally applicable to the present Convention, unless the Parties have otherwise agreed.

ARTICLE 25

Without prejudice to the provisions of articles 22 and 24, the present Convention shall not derogate from Conventions containing provisions on the matters governed by this

des dispositions sur les matières réglées par la présente Convention.

Convention to which the contracting States are, or shall become, Parties.

ARTICLE 26

La présente Convention est ouverte à la signature des Etats représentés à la Dixième session de la Conférence de La Haye de droit international privé.

Elle sera ratifiée et les instruments de ratification seront déposés auprès du Ministère des Affaires Etrangères des Pays-Bas.

ARTICLE 26

The present Convention shall be open for signature by the States represented at the Tenth Session of the Hague Conference on Private International Law.

It shall be ratified, and the instruments of ratification shall be deposited with the Ministry of Foreign Affairs of the Netherlands.

ARTICLE 27

La présente Convention entrera en vigueur le soixantième jour après le dépôt du troisième instrument de ratification prévu par l'article 26, alinéa 2.

La Convention entrera en vigueur, pour chaque Etat signataire ratifiant postérieurement, le soixantième jour après le dépôt de son instrument de ratification.

ARTICLE 27

The present Convention shall enter into force on the sixtieth day after deposit of the third instrument of ratification referred to in the second paragraph of article 26.

The Convention shall enter into force for each signatory State which ratifies subsequently on the sixtieth day after the deposit of its instrument of ratification.

ARTICLE 28

Tout Etat non représenté à la Dixième session de la Conférence de La Haye de droit international privé pourra adhérer à la présente Convention après son entrée en vigueur en vertu de l'article 27, alinéa premier. L'instrument d'adhésion sera déposé auprès du Ministère des Affaires Etrangères des Pays-Bas.

La Convention n'entrera en vigueur pour un tel Etat qu'à défaut d'opposition de la part d'un Etat ayant ratifié la Convention avant ce dépôt, notifiée au Ministère des Affaires Etrangères des Pays-Bas dans un délai de six mois à partir de la date à laquelle ce Ministère lui aura notifié cette adhésion.

A défaut d'opposition, la Convention entrera en vigueur pour l'Etat adhérant le premier jour du mois qui suit l'expiration du dernier des délais mentionnés à l'alinéa précédent.

ARTICLE 28

Any State not represented at the Tenth Session of the Hague Conference on Private International Law may accede to the present Convention after it has entered into force in accordance with the first paragraph of article 27. The instrument of accession shall be deposited with the Ministry of Foreign Affairs of the Netherlands.

The Convention shall enter into force for such a State in the absence of any objection from a State, which has ratified the Convention before such deposit, notified to the Ministry of Foreign Affairs of the Netherlands within a period of six months after the date on which the said Ministry has notified it of such accession.

In the absence of any such objection, the Convention shall enter into force for the acceding State on the first day of the month following the expiration of the last of the periods referred to in the preceding paragraph.

ARTICLE 29

Tout Etat, au moment de la signature, de la ratification ou de l'adhésion, pourra déclarer que la présente Convention s'étendra à l'ensemble des territoires qu'il représente sur le plan international, ou à l'un ou plusieurs

ARTICLE 29

Any State may, at the time of signature, ratification or accession, declare that the present Convention shall extend to all the territories for the international relations of which it is responsible, or to one or more of d'entre eux. Cette déclaration aura effet au moment de l'entrée en vigueur de la Convention pour ledit Etat.

Par la suite, toute extension de cette nature sera notifiée au Ministère des Affaires Etrangères des Pays-Bas.

La Convention entrera en vigueur, pour les territoires visés par l'extension, le soixantième jour après la notification mentionnée à l'alinéa précédent.

them. Such a declaration shall take effect on the date of entry into force of the Convention for the State concerned.

At any time thereafter, such extensions shall be notified to the Ministry of Foreign Affairs of the Netherlands.

The Convention shall enter into force for the territories mentioned in such an extension on the sixtieth day after the notification referred to in the preceding paragraph.

ARTICLE 30

La présente Convention aura une durée de cinq ans à partir de la date de son entrée en vigueur conformément à l'article 27, alinéa premier, même pour les Etats qui l'auront ratifiée ou y auront adhéré postérieurement.

La Convention sera renouvelée tacitement de cinq en cinq ans, sauf dénonciation.

La dénonciation sera, au moins six mois avant l'expiration du délai de cinq ans, notifiée au Ministère des Affaires Etrangères des Pays-Bas.

Elle pourra se limiter à certains des territoires auxquels s'applique la Convention.

La dénonciation n'aura d'effet qu'à l'égard de l'Etat qui l'aura notifiée. La Convention restera en vigueur pour les autres Etats contractants.

ARTICLE 30

The present Convention shall remain in force for five years from the date of its entry into force in accordance with the first paragraph of article 27, even for States which have ratified it or acceded to it subsequently.

If there has been no denunciation, it shall be renewed tacitly every five years.

Any denunciation shall be notified to the Ministry of Foreign Affairs of the Netherlands at least six months before the end of the five year period.

It may be limited to certain of the territories to which the Convention applies.

The denunciation shall have effect only as regards the State which has notified it. The Convention shall remain in force for the other contracting States.

ARTICLE 31

Le Ministère des Affaires Etrangères des Pays-Bas notifiera aux Etats visés à l'article 26, ainsi qu'aux Etats qui auront adhéré conformément aux dispositions de l'article 28:

a) les signatures et ratifications visées à l'article 26;

b) la date à laquelle la présente Convention entrera en vigueur conformément aux dispositions de l'article 27, alinéa premier;

c) les adhésions visées à l'article 28 et la date à laquelle elles auront effet;

d) les extensions visées à l'article 29 et la date à laquelle elles auront effet;

e) les désignations, opposition et déclarations mentionnées à l'article 21;

f) les dénonciations visées à l'article 30, alinéa 3.

ARTICLE 31

The Ministry of Foreign Affairs of the Netherlands shall give notice to the States referred to in article 26, and to the States which have acceded in accordance with article 28, of the following –

(a) the signatures and ratifications referred to in article 26;

(b) the date on which the present Convention enters into force in accordance with the first paragraph of article 27;

(c) the accessions referred to in article 28 and the dates on which they take effect;

(d) the extensions referred to in article 29 and the dates on which they take effect;

(e) the designations, oppositions and declarations referred to in article 21;

(f) the denunciations referred to in the third paragraph of article 30.

En foi de quoi, les soussignés, dûment autorisés, ont signé la présente Convention.

In witness whereof the undersigned, being duly authorised thereto, have signed the present Convention.

Fait à La Haye, le [1] .... 19.., en français et en anglais, les deux textes faisant également foi, en un seul exemplaire, qui sera déposé dans les archives du Gouvernement des Pays-Bas et dont une copie certifiée conforme sera remise, par la voie diplomatique, à chacun des Etats représentés à la Dixième session de la Conférence de La Haye de droit international privé.

Done at The Hague, on the [1] .... day of ...., 19.., in the English and French languages, both texts being equally authentic, in a single copy which shall be deposited in the archives of the Government of the Netherlands, and of which a certified copy shall be sent, through the diplomatic channel, to each of the States represented at the Tenth Session of the Hague Conference on Private International Law.

---

[1] Cette Convention a été ouverte à la signature et signée le 15 novembre 1965 par la République Fédérale d'Allemagne, les Etats-Unis d'Amérique, la Finlande et les Pays-Bas. Elle a été signée également le 25 novembre 1965 par Israël; le 10 décembre 1965 par le Royaume-Uni de Grande-Bretagne et d'Irlande; le 21 janvier 1966 par la Belgique et le 1er mars 1966 par la République Arabe Unie.

The Role of the Government in the Japanese Business Law System   **6**

A key issue today in discussing the Japanese business system is how closely intertwined business and government are. It was supposedly James Abegglen who first coined the term "Japan, Inc." to represent what he perceived as the close, virtually symbiotic relationship between business and government in Japan.[1] Whatever the validity of that term, there clearly does exist in Japan today a great cooperation between government and business, regulator and regulatee.

The Japanese business system is a hybrid unique to Japan of free market and government involvement. Its uniqueness is derived from the way in which the government regulates the economy. In a democracy such as Japan's, economic regulation by the government is usually based on laws authorizing the government through its ministries to regulate the various sectors of the economy. In Japan, though, the governmental ministries often do not apply the laws directly to regulate business but rather use a more informal process, one sometimes based on no statutory authorization at all. The most famous example of this process is "administrative guidance."[2] Administrative guidance is the term used to express the means by which agencies of the Japanese government, especially MITI (Ministry of International Trade and Industry), use nonlegal weapons, weapons for which there is usually no precise statutory authorization, to convince business to act in the way the government desires. The two significant features of administrative guidance to Americans are (1) that it is informal, and (2) that there is usually little, if any, statutory authorization for the ministry to act in the way it does.[3]

In structure, Japan's actual system of government is vastly different from that of the United States, although both are trilateral in organization. The U.S. system, of course, is composed of the executive, judicial, and legislative branches. Japan's though, is made up of the elected politicians, big business, and the higher elements of the bureaucracy.[4] These three groups not only work together in a consensus framework for what is commonly perceived as the good of Japan, but in addition each needs the help of the others. The elected politicians of the Diet (the Japanese legislature), for example, preside over the bureaucrats but also need their help. There are fewer appointive positions in the Japanese government than in Washington; a new election thus does not result in as many sweeping changes in Tokyo. Since Japanese bureaucrats as a consequence rise to higher levels in government than their American counterparts, their role in government becomes more important. Their importance is so great that higher-level bureaucrats often are asked by the political parties to run for the Diet itself.[5] In addition, Japanese bureaucrats are usually the ones who draw up the legislation to be submitted to the Diet. While the elected politicians may suggest laws to them, rarely do the politicians or their staff actually draft the legislation. That task is one for the bureaucrats, thus forging another tie between the members of the Diet and the bureaucracy.

Ties between the politicians and big business are strong, since so much of the funding for election campaigns comes from the coffers of big business. Big business occupies a special role in the Japanese political landscape; one prominent observer of the Japanese scene has called the head of Keidanren, the organization that represents big business in Japan, the prime minister of Japan's "invisible government."[6] The ties are obviously not ones that run just one way: the Diet will have before it many proposed laws that will affect business activities.

The bureaucracy and big business also have close ties under the Japanese system. Before the bureaucracy submits a law to the Diet affecting business, business executives usually will be asked to examine the proposed legislation and make comments. In this way, a consensus for the proposed legislation develops. The ties between the bureaucracy and big business are solidified by personal contacts. Those employed by business and the government often have graduated from the same prestigious university, and these friendships invariably lead to after-working-hours dinners and other social meetings in which conversation on topics of mutual interest take place. During these meetings, businessmen and government officials will exchange views.[7] Often, bureaucrats at the higher levels of government will retire from government service at the age of fifty-five and then go to work for a company involved in the field in which the former bureaucrat worked. The Japanese call this entry into business from the bureaucracy "amakudari," i.e., descent from heaven.[8] The word "heaven" reflects the strong respect and prominence the bureaucracy has in Japan.

The Japanese are very conscious of their need for international trade. Japan possesses few natural resources and little farmable land.[9] To survive—let alone, to prosper—in today's world, Japan must engage in international trade. To the Japanese, international trade is their key to survival.[10] Therefore, big business in the Japanese system plays a key role, since big business forms the keystone of Japan's trade with the world. To help big business in international trade—and thus, ultimately, the nation of Japan itself—the government uses a variety of incentives for big business so that business proceeds along the parameters that the government believes are desirable. This use of incentives is cited by many as evidence of the correctness of the phrase "Japan, Inc."[11]

The Japanese government uses the weapons at its control, these incentives, to compel business to follow the government's desire as to what sectors of business should be emphasized. Business when it follows the government's behest, though, does not act because of the government's statutory powers or its authoritarian control. Rather, the Japanese government, especially MITI and the MOF (Ministry of Finance), employs consultation, advice, persuasion, and even threat to a degree undreamt of in Washington—despite limited statutory powers. The bureaus of MITI, for example, constantly draw up industrial sectoral targets and plans.[12] These plans are not, however, drawn up in a vacuum. Constant consultation goes on between business and government. There are over 300 consulting committees in the Japanese government formed expressly for this purpose.[13]

Under the principal direction of MITI and the Economic Planning Agency, representatives of the bureaucracy, business, academia, media, and other sectors of Japanese society meet and draw up an economic blueprint describing which sectors of the economy will be especially important in the future. Economic incentives are then provided by the government of Japan to induce Japanese companies to help develop these sectors.[14] Again, it must be emphasized that this plan is not a compulsory one for business; it is merely advisory. The Japanese government does not compel businesses to invest in these areas. Rather, it seeks to make it in their interests to do so. The ties that exist between government and business in Japan thus become even closer due to the government's use of these incentives. The "visions" of future industrial development are also significant because they define a national consensus of key trends and thus serve to assist the decision making of private business.

The Japanese Cabinet itself has final approval of this plan. The Diet, though, has no actual role in the formulation or approval of the plan. Instead it is the Japanese bureaucracy that occupies a prominent role in the process—and therefore in the formulation of economic policy in Japan.[15]

There are many incentives available to the Japanese government by which business can be pushed to act in the direction urged by the government through these targets and plans. Those who assert the validity of the term "Japan, Inc." point to these incentives as evidence of the closeness of the business-government relationship in Japan. Some of these incentives are the subsidization of research and development, furnishing of technological information, loans to business, and tax relief.

One prominent example of how the Japanese government can push business in the direction it favors is the subsidization of research and development. Currently, for example, MITI is providing financial aid in the amount of $450 million to several large Japanese companies in their quest to develop the fifth generation computer, i.e., a computer that will be able to perform human-like reasoning.[16] The Tsukuba Science City, a 70,000-acre complex thirty-seven miles northeast of Tokyo, has an annual government budget of $600 million. At Tsukuba, researchers from both private industry and the government work on projects deemed important by the government.[17] In addition to providing research and development subsidies, the government also acts as a national clearinghouse for technological information for export industries.

Another way in which business is moved to follow the Japanese government's plans is by loans. Unlike industry in the United States which is largely shareholder (i.e., equity) financed, Japanese companies are financed largely through bank loans. Through "window guidance" the Japanese government is able to use this credit financing of corporations to push industry to adopt the government's objectives. Acting through the Bank of Japan, a bank controlled by the Ministry of Finance, the government provides credit to banks that conform their loan policy to government priorities.[18] This process is called "window guidance" because through this "window" of credit the government "guides" business policies. In addition, by observing which companies are granted loans by the government-owned Japan Development Bank, the commercial banks can note which industries are favored by the government (Table 6.1 shows which sectors of the economy in Japan have been favored since 1955 by low interest loans from the Japan Development Bank). This source of government support is carefully targeted, particularly on key technologies, and it serves as a signal to private lenders, suppliers, and customers that the industry or project in question is important to Japan's development. Through these methods the Japanese government helps companies in industries targeted for growth to obtain capital. The crucial role of the banks in this targeting process is clearly recognized by the government. When Toyo Kogyo, the maker of Mazda automobiles, was in dire financial straits in the early 1970s, Sumitomo Bank, the major lender to Toyo Kogyo, helped

Table 6.1

Sectors of the Economy Receiving Low Interest Loans from the Japan Development Bank

Sector	1955–1964	1965–1974	1975–Present	Total
Autos	.4	11.9	—	.3
Auto parts	12.4	33.3	20.0	65.7
Semiconductors	2.4	18.5	40.6	61.5
Computers	5.2	184.9	343.4	533.5
Machine tools	6.4	.6	.1	7.1
Steel	11.8	5.6	—	17.4
			Total	697.5

(Unit 1 billion yen)

Source: *Nihon Keizai*, July 7, 1983, at 1, as quoted by *The Japan Law Letter*, July/ August 1983, at 5.

restore it to financial health. According to a recent study, the government's assurance that any losses sustained by Sumitomo Bank in this matter would be alleviated by the granting to it of special government favors played a key role in the bank's decision to preserve the company.[19] Such an assurance is a direct example of how the government uses the banks and their role in corporate financing to push industry to adopt government objectives.

The tax system in Japan is another powerful incentive available to the government as a means to make business follow its plans. Unlike the United States, Japan has a tax system that is far from neutral. Through various taxing measures such as accelerated depreciation, the government provides incentives supporting the development of growth industries.[20] Under one law, for instance, facilities used to produce "newly developed technologies may be depreciated in the first year by an amount equal to one-third of the initial book value of the facilities, in addition to normal depreciation."[21] The end result of such tax benefits is that Japanese companies, by pursuing the policy advocated by the government, gain an enormous cash flow advantage over their foreign competitors.

Of all the measures available to the Japanese government to encourage business to act at its direction, the most powerful is administrative guidance. Administrative guidance, as mentioned earlier, is a tool unique to the Japanese system. Its uniqueness is due to the high degree of compliance obtained by a ministry of the Japanese government through its "requests" to industry even though its legal authority to act is frequently questionable at best.[22]

There are various types of administrative guidance. The three main ones are promotional administrative guidance, adjudicatory administrative guidance, and regulatory administrative guidance.[23] In the first, governmental agencies give advice or protection to businesses to promote the enterprises' own interests. In the second, governmental agencies usurp the role of the courts and help businesses to resolve disputes. In the third, agencies such as MITI in lieu of issuing orders based on a statutory authority to regulate businesses will instead issue "recommendations." Often, there is no legal basis at all for such a recommendation. One example of administrative guidance in this area particularly important to foreign business is the Dow Chemical case. Dow, a leading U.S. chemical company, announced plans to produce caustic soda in Japan. There was no legal reason to prevent Dow from so proceeding. MITI, however, fearful that Dow's entry into this economic sector would damage the industry in Japan, negotiated with Dow an agreement whereby Dow agreed to a limit on its production in Japan of caustic soda. The importance of this case is that, despite the absence of any legal basis for its action, MITI suggested that Dow limit its entry into the Japanese market—and Dow acceded to this request.[24]

In its broadest sense then, administrative guidance is a process for which there is no statutory authorization. It is a request to business by a ministry of the Japanese government for voluntary cooperation. In America, such a request would not readily be heeded by business. Yet, in Japan these requests are invariably followed even though from a legal viewpoint the requested party is entirely free not to comply. The crucial question is, of course, why.

The most important reason why business adheres so closely to the suggestions of the Japanese governmental ministries, especially those of MITI, is actually an intertwining of two. One reason is that both the bureaucracy and business are on fundamentals in such sufficient agreement that a consensus can be struck. As Professor Lockwood has written, "their values are mostly in common and their attitudes instrumental."[25] At the same time, though, business is cognizant of the power of such agencies as MITI (see Table 6.2 for a breakdown of MITI's basic organization). The precedent is clear that one defies their wishes, even those without any legal authorization, at great peril. The example of Sumitomo's defiance of MITI in the mid-1960s makes this point clear.

Iron and steel market conditions in Japan had declined considerably in 1965. MITI officials believed that drastic counter measures were necessary, but the laws of Japan gave MITI no authority for regulating iron and steel production. Therefore, MITI searched for any justification it could find to limit iron and steel production in Japan in order to improve the prospects for those companies involved in these areas. For lack of a more specific authorization, MITI seized on the general

Table 6.2
Basic Organization of the Ministry of International Trade and Industry

International Trade Policy Bureau	International Trade Administration Bureau	Industrial Policy Bureau
The Americas-Oceania	Exports	Research
West Europe-Africa-Middle East	Imports	Industrial Structure
South Asia-East Europe	Agricultural and Marine Products	Industrial Finance
North Asia	Foreign Exchange and Trade Finance	Business Behavior
Trade Research	Export Insurance and Planning	International Enterprise
International Economic Affairs	Long-Term Export Insurance	Commercial Policy
Economic Cooperation	Short-Term Export Insurance	Commercial Affairs
		Price Policy

Basic Industries Bureau

Iron and Steel Administration
Iron and Steel Production
Nonferrous Metals
Basic Chemical Products
Chemical Products Safety
Chemical Fertilizers
Alcohol Industry

Machinery and Information Industries Bureau	Industrial Location and Environmental Protection Bureau	Consumer Goods Industries Bureau
International Trade	Industrial Relocation	International Trade
Industrial Machinery	Industrial Location Guidance	Fiber and Spinning
Cast and Forged Products	Industrial Water	Textile Products
Electronics Policy	Environmental Protection Planning	Paper and Pulp Industry
Data Processing	Environmental Protection Guidance	Household Goods
Electronics and Electrical Machinery	Industrial Safety	Recreational Goods
Automobiles		Ceramics and Construction Materials
Aircraft and Ordnance		Housing Industry
Other Vehicles		Textile Inspection Administrator
Weights and Measures		
Machinery Credit Insurance		

Source: Steve Lohr, "Japan's Trade Ministry Draws Praise and Ire," *The New York Times*, May 17, 1983, at 44.

provisions of its organizational law to argue that it could act in this regard. That law delegates to MITI the responsibility of promoting the production of export goods and promoting, improving, and regulating the production, circulation, and consumption of industrial goods.[26] To the eighty-five companies involved, MITI, *inter alia*, issued "suggestions" that the companies should limit their production. Market conditions, however, failed to improve, and so on November 13, 1965, each Japanese company involved was given explicit instructions by MITI as to its production volume limit. One company, Sumitomo Metal Mining Company, refused to comply with the recommendation that it lower its production. Sumitomo contended that such a request was an interference in the company's own rights. The people at MITI refused to change their position. To intensify pressure on Sumitomo Metal Mining Company to adhere to its recommendation, MITI went so far as to curtail Sumitomo's foreign coal import quota. Finally, on September 11, 1966, the matter was settled by the two entities.[27]

MITI's action in the case is considered especially significant by the Japanese in two respects. One is that it showed that MITI would not hesitate to use the very general parameters of its 1952 organizational law as a basis for any suggestion it might care to offer to Japanese business. The statute gives to MITI the duty to promote the production of export goods and the promotion, improvement, and regulation of industrial goods.[28] The general nature of that language in its broadest interpretation is such as to give virtually unfettered power over the Japanese economy to MITI, an interpretation usually favored by MITI. The second point of the case was the ferocity of MITI's anger and vengeful nature when its "suggestion" was not obeyed. Sumitomo had failed to comply with MITI's request that it (along with eighty-four other companies) lower its production. Even though this suggestion was just that, i.e., not an order authorized by law, MITI, once defied by Sumitomo Metal as to iron and steel production limits, immediately used the broad interpretation of its organizational law to punish the company severely in another area by limiting the amount of foreign coal it could import. The lesson was not lost on business in Japan: defiance of MITI was a risky move indeed, since the ministry would not hesitate to punish a company in any area of the economy.

In 1969, MITI's image of itself as all-powerful in Japan became even more pronounced. In that year, an industrial exhibit was to be held in the Chinese cities of Shanghai and Bejing to promote trade among Japan, China, the USSR, and other socialist nations. A Japanese group applied to MITI for permission to export to the show about 3,000 items for display. As to nineteen of them, MITI adopted a "disapproval disposition." The plaintiff sued MITI in a suit called by many the *Cocom Case*, contending its action was illegal.[29] The Tokyo District Court agreed. After the decision was announced, MITI issued the following statement:

In today's decision, in its reasoning, the Court stated that the restriction of exports by the agreement of the Coordinating Committee was illegal. However, the Ministry of International Trade and Industry believes that this kind of export restriction is without doubt legal since it is done based on [appropriate] Laws and Orders in order to plan the sound development of our country's international trade and national economy. Therefore, from this time on, the Government will adopt the same policy as before.[30]

This pronouncement by MITI is important in that it reveals how omnipotent MITI believes itself to be. For MITI to say publicly that it has read the court's decision declaring it to have acted wrongly, does not agree with it, and therefore will continue acting as it has before shows not only that MITI believes its judgment in economic matters should be followed by all without question but also that the opinion of the court is not the final determinant. To MITI, its opinion is the one that matters—and the one it will follow. That same attitude is seen also in the *Sumitomo Case* where MITI acted to punish the company by lowering its coal import amount because the company did not follow MITI's "suggestion" that it decrease its production limit of iron and steel.

In both the *Cocom* and *Sumitomo Cases*, MITI interpreted the applicable statutes in the way that would give the ministry the most power available. MITI has done so in many other instances to push business to the policies it deems most beneficial to the Japanese economy. Japan's Antimonopoly Law, for instance, exempts or excludes from its prohibitions depression cartels and certain export cartels. Influential spokesmen for MITI acting under the aegis of this law have often in the past openly pressed for cartels. Decrying what they termed "excessive" competition, they asserted that cartelization was needed so that Japanese companies could act more efficiently against their foreign competition. Nonetheless, their advice has been ignored by some Japanese companies. In the 1960s, MITI actually tried to persuade ten automakers in Japan to merge into Toyota and Nissan. MITI argued that the automobile industry in Japan would function better if it were dominated by a few big firms that could reap the benefits of large-scale production. Only one company complied.[31] Later, MITI tried to keep Honda, then a motorcycle firm only, out of the auto business. The founder of Honda, Soichiro Honda, defied the ministry and built it into Japan's third largest auto producer.[32] These examples of defiance, once infrequent, have become more common. Now that many Japanese companies have become front-runners in global markets, they have less incentive to cooperate not only with other Japanese companies but also with the government itself.

In the area of international trade, MITI's power over business is virtually without parameters due to two laws, the Export Trade Control Order[33] and the Export and Import Transactions Law (Transactions Law).[34] The Export Trade Control Order states that "[a]ny person desiring to export goods which fall into [certain classes] shall obtain the written approval" of MITI and declares that MITI can forbid or attach conditions to the granting of a license when it decides doing so is necessary "for the maintenance of the balance of international payments and the sound development of international trade or the national economy."[35] The purpose of the Transactions Law is to ensure order in export and import transactions; the agency charged with the maintenance of such order is, of course, MITI.[36]

The importance of the two laws is that since they are both administered by MITI they are used by MITI as policy instruments to achieve its international trade objectives. One prominent Japanese professor has, for example, written that MITI basically regulates Japanese exports through export cartels and export associations based on the Transactions Law.[37] That statement is certainly a strong one, but the fact remains that the Transactions Law does allow two different types of Japanese export cartels. One type of cartel is created by an agreement among exporters or manufacturers of commodities to be exported, and the other is one in which an export association stipulates matters to be obeyed by its members. The law itself states that those wishing to form a cartel for foreign exports must inform MITI at least ten days before the agreement's conclusion.[38] MITI must issue an order amending or prohibiting the agreement if it violates one of several conditions, such as it harms importers or dealers in the country of destination or it hampers the development of export trade.[39]

Thus, the Export Trade Control Order establishes in Japan a compulsory system of export licensing while the Transactions Law permits export agreements among private enterprises, with MITI being the enforcement agency for both statutes. MITI, though, has interpreted the statutes as legislation empowering the ministry to take the initiative and order private companies to enter into compulsory export agreements. This claimed power is not a lightly exercised one, either. According to one recent study, "Japan has a far higher rate of export by cartels than do most other advanced nations."[40]

MITI has not been reticent about its claim to exercise this power. In 1975, for instance, it made the following statement to the U.S. Department of State:

MITI will exercise its powers provided for in the Export Trade Control Law ... [and] under the Foreign Exchange and Foreign Trade Control Law, without prior direction to the industry or trade associations to enter into such arrangements.

... [S]uch Arrangements concluded under the Export and Import [Transactions] Law and carried out under the direction of the Minister of International Trade and Industry in order to assure orderly Japanese exportation activities are the actual implementation of MITI's trade policy itself. And since such direction by MITI, if disregarded, can be enforced by the power pursuant to [the Export Trade Control Order] it has in fact a compulsory power equivalent to law.

Once MITI has decided upon the trade policy measures to be taken and has directed the establishment of appropriate Arrangements under the Export and Import [Transactions] Law for this purpose, the Japanese industries involved have in fact no alternative but to establish them. Therefore, the Arrangements entered into under the Export and Import [Transactions] Law in compliance with the direction of MITI are not private agreements in effect and no less than the implementation of the foreign trade policy of MITI.[41]

This statement by MITI was sent to the State Department for transmittal to the court in a case involving several Japanese television manufacturers. They had been sued in the United States by American television manufacturers on the grounds that the Japanese had acted in violation of U.S. antitrust law. MITI's statement was issued to support the defense of the Japanese companies.[42] MITI also declared that it had not only directed the Japanese television manufacturers to fix minimum prices for export but in addition supervised the preparation of the agreement and regulated the parties involved. To show how far MITI believes its powers to run, the statement continued as follows:

Had the Japanese television manufacturers and exporters failed to comply with MITI's direction to establish such an agreement or regulation, MITI would have invoked its powers provided for in the Export Trade Control Law in order to unilaterally control television sales for export to the United States and carry out its established trade policy.[43]

Thus, MITI has one more powerful weapon in its vast arsenal. If in the unlikely situation its direction of the Japanese economy through administrative guidance proves insufficient, MITI will exercise the power it has arrogated to itself under a very strained reading of the Transactions Law and Export Trade Control Order so that its trade policy is implemented.

As the maestro that organizes Japanese industrial policy, MITI not only acts to help Japanese companies increase sales, MITI also oversees the contraction of Japanese industries deemed not to be competitive internationally and having excess production capacity. After discussion and review, companies in such industries collectively scrap a certain percentage of their surplus plant and equipment. The petrochemical industry is one current example of the paring of business in Japan.

The twelve main producers recently reached an agreement to cut capacity 36 percent by early 1985.[44]

The use in Japan of government incentives and directives to help bolster important industries has not gone unnoticed in the United States. Indeed, the reverse is true. Many American politicians and business executives now urge the United States government to follow the example of "Japan, Inc." and subsidize industries it thinks will succeed.[45] They argue that central planning is responsible for Japan's success. Such recent works as Chalmers Johnson's *MITI and the Japanese Miracle*[46] declare that Japan's postwar economic success is largely due to MITI's masterminding of the Japanese economy through the nurturing and directing of Japan's industry with subsidies and cartels. For years, these people assert, Japan has been "targeting" individual industries, giving them special breaks to compete in the United States and other markets. If it works for the Japanese, proponents ask, why not try it in the United States? Even the Reagan Administration, a great supporter of capitalism and free trade in their most pristine senses, has adopted this view. In 1982, President Reagan announced that the administration would send to Congress legislation to establish a new governmental department, the Department of International Trade and Industry (DITI), a sort of U.S. counterpart to MITI, to help U.S. industry compete more effectively in world markets. For a similar reason, Attorney General William French Smith advocated the relaxing of antitrust restrictions to allow high technology American companies to pool their resources in competing for research and development contracts.[47]

Those who contend that the United States should adopt an industrial policy of its own similar to that in Japan are ignoring, I believe, some of the cultural features of the system idiosyncratic to the Japanese that make the system so successful there. Such factors as the high respect accorded to the bureaucracy, the key role of the elite bureaucrats, the virtual unity of values and attitudes in Japan between government and business, and the unwillingness of business to contest government "suggestions" in court as to what course of action it should adopt all contribute in strong measure to the enormous success of Japan's industrial policy. The absence of these factors in the U.S. system, though, makes the transplanting to the United States of Japan's national industrial policy system extremely difficult. In addition, a variety of other factors have contributed to Japan's economic success. Some of them are the influence of Confucianism[48] in the Japanese culture which encourages, *inter alia*, hard work and thrift; low taxes;[49] high savings rate;[50] low unemployment; less restrictive antitrust laws;[51] the commitment to quality control; and the ease, by and large, with which the Japanese have been able so far to borrow technology from abroad rather than spending huge sums on its development themselves.

For the United States to adopt Japan's national industrial policy system and its concomitant features would violate some of our most basic principles. Administrative guidance as it is practiced in Japan most likely would be unconstitutional here. For the government to favor some industries while urging others to scale down their operations due to their lack of competitiveness would violate our strict constitutional requirements of separation of powers and due process. Even more fundamentally, the underpinnings of our constitutional system would not tolerate a concept of government largesse that is available to some companies but not others.

Some features of the Japanese system, however, not only could be adopted by the United States but should be. The Japanese example of how well a system can work when there is a fundamental consensus between government and business is a shining beacon that should light the way. For too long business has regarded government in the United States as a necessary cost of doing business while government has looked at business with distaste. Their relationship should not be inherently and constantly adversarial. Just as business and government in Japan often put aside what is good for each individually and concentrate on what will truly help the nation itself in the long run, so should a similar course become more frequent in the United States.[52] Government and business as well as other groups must arrive at a recognized and shared set of policy goals for the economy and the nation.

Second, as do the Japanese, the United States must emphasize exports. The enactment of legislation in late 1982 that finally allows U.S. companies to establish trading companies is an important step in this regard.[53] Rather than focusing on import restrictions to help such industries as the automobile one, the United States should concentrate first on identifying sectors in which it has a comparative advantage and then identify the ways by which the government can help them to improve export performance. What the United States really needs is an industrial policy that will both aid those industries which are strong and alleviate the dysfunctions that will occur if the government stops protecting those sectors where in the world market the United States has no competitive advantage. Uniform treatment of industry by the U.S. government must end. In a manner similar to the Japanese example, the U.S. government must supply additional research and development aid, tax benefits, and financing to stimulate productivity by those sectors of the economy that provide the greatest opportunity for our competitive advantage in the international marketplace.

The entrepreneurial climate for industry must, in addition, be enhanced. The process itself must be targeted, as well as specific industries. Research and development capabilities, the foundation of high-technology products, must be improved. To accomplish this end, antitrust laws must be revised to allow joint research and development projects; federal funding of basic research and development at the university level should be increased; and a technology-oriented tax scheme should be enacted to lower capital gains taxes, extend R & D tax credits, and give favorable tax treatment to encourage risk-taking by entrepreneurs.

Finally, if the U.S. government is not only to establish economic goals for the country but in addition to give business the incentives that will help achieve them, government itself must be staffed with professionals who possess the same type of superb education, intelligence, and overall ability as the bureaucrats of Japan. What is needed is not political patronage but expertise and a commitment to the position so that an effective industrial policy can be formed and then achieved. I do not mean to say that the United States lacks people in the government who possess these qualities but rather that these people must be put in the fore so that the U.S. position in the international marketplace is strengthened.

NOTES

1. *See* J. Abegglen, *The Japanese Factory: Aspects of Its Social Organization* (1958).

2. In the last few years, there has been much written on the topic of administrative guidance. Some of the better articles are Matsushita, "Administrative Guidance," and Economic Regulation in Japan," 1 *The Japan Business Law Journal* 209 (December 1980); Yamanouchi, "Administrative Guidance and the Role of Law," 7 *Law in Japan: An Annual* 22 (1974); Narita, "Administrative Guidance," 2 *Law in Japan: An Annual* 45 (1968).

3. It could be argued that the use of "jawboning" by Presidents of the United States resembles administrative guidance. The two differ considerably, however, in that administrative guidance is much more pervasive and common in its use in Japan than any comparable activity of the government in the United States including jawboning.

4. The word "bureaucrat" to the Japanese does not at all have the negative connotations it does to Americans. In fact, the opposite is true. A prize job in Japan is working for the Foreign Ministry, Ministry of Finance, or Ministry of International Trade. A story often heard in Japan is that when a son is born the mother fervently hopes that he will go to the University of Tokyo and then enter the government. How many American mothers when their child is born earnestly desire that the child will become a bureaucrat?

5. About a third, for example, of the members of the LDP (Liberal Democratic Party, the party that controls the Japanese government) in the Diet at present are former bureaucrats. Mike Tharp, "Coming Home to Roost," *Far Eastern Economic Review*, September 29, 1983, at 30.

6. D. Henderson, *Foreign Enterprise in Japan* 57 (1973).

7. P. Trezise and Y. Suzuki, "Politics, Government, and Economic Growth

in Japan," in *Asia's New Giant,* H. Patrick and H. Rosovsky, eds. 769 (1976). These "informal" meetings play a crucial role in the Japanese business system.

8. This "descent" is common. In April of 1983, for instance, thirty-two officials of MITI alone made it. Steve Lohr, "Japan's Trade Ministry Draws Praise and Ire," *The New York Times,* May 17, 1983, at 1, 44.

9. Only about 15 percent of Japan's land area is under cultivation. The soils of Japan, moreover, are on the whole not very fertile. *See, e.g.,* E. Reischauer, *The Japanese* 16 (1977).

10. Former MITI Vice Minister for International Affairs Naohiro Amaya is one of many who argue that Japan had little choice but to become a trading nation. "Having no resources of our own," he recently declared, "we had to buy food and other raw materials from overseas and then export the bulk of our production to pay for more imports. Imports, exports, and internationalization have been a means of survival rather than a conscious choice of lifestyles." "Japan's Survival as a Trading Nation: Learning from Medieval Venice," 2 *Journal of Japanese Trade and Industry* 32 (September/ October 1983).

11. *See, e.g.,* Helen Bendix, "Interaction of Business and Government in Japan: Lessons for the United States," 7, a paper given at the Federal Bar Association Conference on Japan in Washington, D.C. (Fall 1980).

12. The broadest plans for shifts in Japan's industrial structure appear in the ten-year forecasts prepared by MITI. These plans are called "visions." The most recent was published in March of 1980. Lohr, *supra* note 8, at 44.

13. Lockwood, "Japan's New Capitalism," in *The State and Economic Enterprise in Japan* 495, 501 (W. Lockwood ed. 1965).

14. Recently, for example, several Japanese companies at the request of MITI have worked on the development of a new computer that can "think," labeled by many the Fifth Generation Computer. *See, e.g.,* E. Feigenbaum and P. McCorduck, *The Fifth Generation* (1983).

15. *See, e.g.,* T. Hattori and D. Henderson, *Civil Procedure in Japan,* 1-23 (1983).

16. *See, e.g.,* "Computers," *Time,* August 1, 1983, at 57.

17. "Science," *Time,* August 1, 1983, at 56.

18. For an excellent discussion of the role of the Bank of Japan, *see,* "Bank of Japan," in T. Adams and I. Hoshii, *A Financial History of the New Japan* 99-104 (1972).

19. Pascale and Rohlen, "The Mazda Turnaround," in 9 *Journal of Japanese Studies* 219, 231 (Summer 1983).

20. Y. Gomi, *Guide to Japanese Taxes* 179-182 (1980).

21. Such tax benefits as those discussed in the text are more fully described in Report of the Comptroller General of the United States, *United States-Japan Trade: Issues and Problems* 178-182 (1979).

22. *See, e.g.,* Ramseyer, "Japanese Antitrust Enforcement After the Oil Embargo," 31 *Am. J. Comp. L.* 395, 397 n.8 (1983).

23. *See, e.g.,* Matsushita, *supra* note 2, at 210.

24. *Id.,* at 212.

25. Lockwood, *supra* note 13, at 502.

26. Ministry of International Trade and Industry Organizational Law, Art. 3 (1)(ii) (Law No. 275, 1952).

27. Narita, *supra* note 2, at 58.

28. *See infra* note 26 and the accompanying text.

29. *1969 Pekin-Shanghai Nihon Kogyo Tenrankai v. Nihon (Cocom Case)*, 20 Gyosei Reishu 842 (Tokyo Dist. Ct., 1969).

30. Quoted in K. Yamauchi, "About the Cocom Decision," 434 *Jurisuto* (Jurist) 71 (1969).

31. "Economy and Business," *Time*, August 1, 1983, at 38, 40.

32. *Id.*

33. Yashutsu boekikanrirei (Export Trade Control Order), Cabinet Order No. 378 of 1949, *translated* in 5 EHS Law Bulletin Series AJ-2.

34. Yushutsunyu torihiki ho (Export and Import Transactions Law), Law No. 299 of 1952, as amended (1965), translated in 1974 *Japan Foreign Trade News* (spec. ed. 348-73).

35. Export Trade Control Order, *supra* note 33, Art. 1.

36. Transactions Law, *supra* note 34, Art. 1.

37. Matsushita, "Export Control and Export Cartels in Japan," 20 *Harvard Int'l L.J.* 103, 110 (1979).

38. Transactions Law, *supra* note 34, Art. 5(1)

39. *Id.*, Art. 5(2).

40. Matsushita, *supra* note 37, at 114.

41. Note from the Japanese government to the State Department (April 25, 1975), 4, duly transmitted by the State Department to the United States District Court for the Eastern District of Pennsylvania and filed in *In re Japanese Elec. Prod. Antitrust Litigation*, 388 F. Supp. 565 (J.P.M.D.L. 1975) [hereinafter Note], *rev'd*, 723 F.2d 238 (3d. Cir. 1983).

42. The defense of the Japanese companies was based on the "act of state doctrine," a judgment of U.S. courts not to adjudicate the legality of the act in question if it was done within a foreign nation's borders and was the public act of those in the foreign nation with authority to exercise sovereign power. *See, e.g.*, E. Hahn, "*Dunhill v. Republic of Cuba*: A Reformulation of the Act of State Defense," 11 *U.W.L.A.L. Rev.* 15 (1979).

43. Note, *supra* note 41, at 5-6.

44. Lohr, "How Japan Helps Its Industry," *The New York Times*, May 18, 1983, at 25, 41.

45. The American press has been awash lately with articles on this subject. *See, e.g.*, Art Pine, "The Outline," *The Wall Street Journal*, September 19, 1983, at 1; D. Henderson, "A Difference of Opinion," *Fortune International*, August 8, 1983, at 113; Steve Lohr, "How Japan Helps Its Industry," *The New York Times*, May 18, 1983, at 25; Steve Lohr, "Japan's Trade Ministry Draws Praise and Ire," *The New York Times*, May 17, 1983, at 1.

46. C. Johnson, *MITI and the Japanese Miracle* (1982).

47. "Smith Acts to Expand R & D Bidding Pool," *The Los Angeles Times*, September 21, 1983, Part IV (Business), at 1.

48. In *The Eastasia Edge*, Roy Hofheinz and Kent Calder argue that the values of Confucianism shared by the Eastasian nations have contributed to the enormous economic success enjoyed by most of them recently. R. Hofheinz and K. Calder, *The Eastasian Edge* 41-52 (1982).

49. From 1951 to 1970, Japan's real gross national product grew at an

average rate of 9 percent per year. During the same period, total national and local taxes (not including social security) dropped from 22.4 percent of national income to 18.9 percent. In the United States, on the other hand, the percentage rose to 31.3 percent from 28.5 percent. D. Henderson, "A Difference of Opinion," *Fortune International*, August 8, 1983, at 113, 114.

50. In 1980, savings in Japan were 19.4 percent of personal income, more than three times the American rate. This high savings percentage leads to capital formation, thus spurring economic growth. *Id.*, at 114.

51. Japan's antitrust statutes are far less restrictive than corresponding U.S. laws on such matters as joint research and development (so that Japanese companies can avoid duplicating the research of others) and mergers.

52. In the fall of 1982, Reps. Timothy Wirth of Colorado and Richard Gaphardt of Missouri wrote a pamphlet in which they made this same point. *See*, "Washington Grapples With Japan's Industrial Policy," *JEI Report #15A*, April 22, 1983, at 1, 6.

53. Export Trading Act of 1982, Pub. L. No. 97-290, 96 Stat. 1233 (1982). For more information about trading companies, *see infra* text accompanying Chapter 4 notes 10-26.

Antitrust in Japan   7

Due to the great publicity given in the U.S. media to Japan's industrial policy, most Americans assume that Japan either has no antitrust laws or has totally ineffective ones. That statement is simply not true today.

It is true that antitrust was an almost unknown policy to the Japanese before the close of World War II. In fact, prior to 1945 Japan had no antitrust laws at all. Cartels were permitted, and there were no legal barriers to the concentration of industrial, commercial, and financial assets.[1] Actual monopolies were rare, but a few tightly controlled, family-concentrated holding companies did dominate Japan's economy. These conglomerates, called "zaibatsu," were unique to Japan. Each family combine tended to operate in a number of markets, in some of which it was strong and in others weak. In these circumstances, competition in one market might easily lead to retaliation in another and thus ultimately to unrestrained economic warfare. This situation placed a premium on the achievement of stability through cartels and organizations.[2]

By the end of World War II the big four zaibatsu (Mitsubishi, Mitsui, Sumitomo, and Yasuda) controlled 49.7 percent of capital in finance, 32.4 percent of total capital in heavy industry, and 24.5 percent of total corporate and partnership capital in Japan.[3] SCAP (Supreme Commander for the Allied Powers) examined this heavy concentration of economic power in a few tightly controlled holding companies and decided that it was a cause of Japan's militarism in the 1930s and 1940s. Therefore, SCAP directives were issued with the intent of dissolving the zaibatsu and fostering policies to promote and maintain competition in Japanese industry.[4]

To ensure that a revival of the concentrated economic power of the zaibatsu would not take place, the Diet in 1947 enacted the Law Relating to Prohibition of Private Monopoly and Methods of Preserving Fair

Trade (called the Antimonopoly Law).[5] Originally based on provisions of such U.S. antitrust statutes as the Sherman, Clayton, and Federal Trade Commission Acts (and the United States courts' interpretation of those acts),[6] the Japanese law prohibited monopolization[7] and unreasonable restraint of trade by cartels which fixed prices, limited quantities, or limited access to technology, facilities, supplies, or the output market.[8] The law further provided that even corporations without a monopoly position could be dismembered if they were found to have an unduly disproportionate bargaining power in a market.[9] In addition, the act prohibited such specified unfair methods of competition as the refusal to receive or supply goods, charging of unduly discriminatory prices or unduly low prices (with the intent to eliminate competitors), coercing of customers to deal exclusively, use of resale price maintenance, and establishment of sole agency contracts.[10] Detailed rules were also set forth governing mergers, interlocking directorates, and intercorporate shareholdings in order to forestall the establishment of monopolies or the recreation of the enormous zaibatsu conglomerates.

To enforce the provisions of the Antimonopoly Law, the Japan Fair Trade Commission was established in the statute itself.[11] This novel administrative and quasi-judicial body is independent of all ministries and administratively responsible directly to the Prime Minister.[12] Its novelty is due to its functions: it combines those of both the Antitrust Division of the U.S. Department of Justice and the Federal Trade Commission. Its members are selected by the Prime Minister, today with the consent of both houses of the Diet.[13] The JFTC (JFTC is the abbreviation commonly used for the Japan Fair Trade Commission so as to avoid confusing it with the Federal Trade Commission of the United States) has primary jurisdiction to administer antitrust laws in Japan. The JFTC does not, though, have cabinet rank; therefore, it is not regarded by most Japanese as being as powerful as those ministries in Japan which are responsible for economic regulation and applications of administrative guidance, such as MITI. Decisions of the JFTC are appealable as a matter of first instance to the Tokyo High Court.[14]

In addition to the JFTC, the Antimonopoly Act provided for private antitrust actions and possible criminal prosecution.[15] Japanese law further provides under Civil Code Article 709 that private parties may bring damage actions for general tort damages arising from a restraint of trade in Japan where there has been no final action by the JFTC. These provisions, though, have proven to be ineffectual. Virtually all of the antitrust suits in Japan have been initiated by the JFTC. One reason for the lack of private antitrust suits in Japan is the absence in Japan, unlike the case in the United States, of treble damages for victorious private plaintiffs.[16] Private actions under the civil code are also rare. Japanese prohibitions against class action suits for damages, the limited scope of discovery available in Japan, the difficulty of satisfying legal proof of violations and damages, and the high cost of bringing a lawsuit in Japan due to its protracted stages of trial are all factors that suggest that private suits under the civil code will, as was true before, not be an active force in Japanese antitrust law enforcement in the future.

Since its enactment in 1947, the Antimonopoly Law has undergone several revisions. In 1949, the law was amended in a way that severely weakened its original provisions. Intercorporate stock ownership which had previously been made illegal to prevent the reoccurrence of zaibatsu-like conglomerates was made legal, the rules on mergers and acquisitions were eased, and restrictions on interlocking directorates were relaxed. In addition, the JFTC's permission power over mergers was lessened to a prior reporting requirement.

In 1953, more substantial revisions of the Antimonopoly Law again took place, and this time also the original thrust of the law was weakened.[17] Corporate breakup for reasons of disparity in bargaining power was eliminated, resale price maintenance was permitted in specified instances, certain types of cartels became legal, and restrictions on interlocking directorships and intercorporate stockholding eased even further. The Antimonopoly Law, as amended in 1953, formed the basis for government antitrust policy in Japan until 1977, when, as we shall see, its provisions were strengthened.

MITI in 1965 suggested the enactment of legislation which would have tremendously increased its power to use administrative guidance in certain areas of the economy. The ministry recommended that it be given the authority to grant exceptions to the Antimonopoly Law and to devise consensus decisions on structural changes in industry. Although this bill was defeated in the Diet, the thrust of MITI's act is significant.[18] The law would have weakened considerably free markets in Japan and made the JFTC virtually useless. This instance of MITI attempting to flex its muscle to diminish freedom of competition in Japan and the role of the JFTC in preserving that freedom is not an atypical one. Since the enactment of the Antimonopoly Law in 1947, MITI and the JFTC, two agencies of the same government, have clashed on several occasions concerning their views of how competitive the marketplace in Japan should be. Until recently, MITI, as we saw in the last chapter, as the principal maestro of industrial policy in Japan, clearly held the upper hand. Such recent actions as the oil cartel litigation of 1980 may, however, presage a different turn of events.[19]

The long trend toward weakening the original intent of the Antimonopoly Law was finally reversed in 1977 by the enactment of an amendment to strengthen the law. As inflation increased in Japan, public attitudes toward collusive industry actions hardened. This industrial cooperation and collusion tended to raise prices thus aggravating the inflation, so that less administrative approval of collusion and stronger antitrust enforcement become more desirable.[20] Besides problems of inflation, shortages of some raw materials and such consumer necessities as toilet paper appeared in 1973 (even prior to the enormous disruption of oil suppliers later in the same year in Japan due to the Arab oil embargo) bringing public outcries of corporate collusion.[21] In response to this public outcry, the JFTC drafted an amendment to the Antimonopoly Law, and it became law in 1977.

The 1977 amendment included within it a number of major changes to the previous law. One change is that the JFTC was authorized to order corporate dissolution or even divestiture if concentration in a market is accompanied by barriers to entry, lack of downward price movements, and unusually high profits. In the second major change, banks' allowable holding of another company's stock was reduced to 5 percent from 10. The third change involved incipient cartels. Firms in an industry must now explain to the JFTC when "harmonious" price increases occur within three months of each other the reasons for the increase. Finally, fines for Antimonopoly Law violations were raised tenfold from ¥ 500,000 to ¥ 5,000,000 (today, about $21,000). Although the amount of the fine is small by U.S. standards, it still represents a significant increase. The most important change in the law, though, may be a psychological one. After years of weakening of the Antimonopoly Law, more teeth were finally put into its features. In addition, the JFTC as an organization received a much-needed transfusion of increased power.

In its operation, the JFTC functions much like the Federal Trade Commission of the United States. Investigations by the JFTC originate in one of three ways: follow-up of complaints filed by private persons, violation reports from the Procurator General, or independent initiation of investigations by the JFTC staff. Once the JFTC has investigated and found the existence of a violation, the case may be settled in one of several ways. The JFTC may issue a recommendation finding, indicating what voluntary measures can be taken to remedy the violation. If the recommendation finding is not followed, formal proceedings are instituted during which the JFTC acts as a tribunal and hands down a formal decision after hearing arguments from its staff and the defendant(s).[22] The defendants may accept a consent decree, though, before the formal decision is reached. Formal decisions, as we have seen before, may also be appealed to the Tokyo High Court(the procedures are charted in Figure 7.1).[23]

Most JFTC rulings have been either recommendations or consent decrees. As Table 7.1 shows, from 1947 to 1981, 612 out of 751 cases were settled by either a recommendation finding or a consent decree.

Figure 7.1
A Flow Chart of the Japanese Antimonopoly Procedures

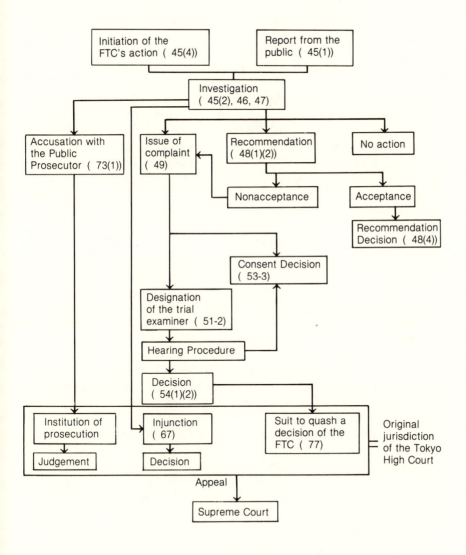

The numbers in parentheses refer to the applicable sections of the Antimonopoly Act.

Only 99 cases went as far as a formal decision (of that number, 18 were appealed to the Tokyo High Court). These figures are actually not as surprising as they might on first glance seem, since the tendency for cases to end with a recommendation or consent decree is entirely in consonance with the general tendency in Japan to avoid courtroom confrontation. Professor John Haley of the University of Washington has suggested that another reason why so few cases brought by the JFTC are litigated by corporate defendants may be due to their fear of adverse publicity. A quick agreement to cease the alleged illegal activity without a formal admission of guilt may to a Japanese corporation be far preferable to a protracted struggle in court with the resultant publicity.[24]

One reason why most Americans have an image of Japan as a country with a lax antitrust policy was the elimination from the original Antimonopoly Law of the per se illegality of cartels.[25] Under the 1953 revision of the statute, recession and rationalization cartels could be authorized by the JFTC.[26] Recession cartels are allowed for limited periods of time of generally six months to one year (although extensions can be granted) whenever an industry faces a decline in business or a price decline serious enough to threaten the continued operation of a majority of the companies in the industrial sector. The JFTC may also approve rationalization cartels in order to coordinate and protect firms in an industry that are investing in facilities needed for more efficient production. Membership in the cartel in both cases is voluntary; the government is not permitted to coerce companies to join the cartels. Neither type of legal cartel has been heavily used. Since 1975, for example, the number of recession cartels used in Japan has been one to six per year, while the number of rationalization cartels has usually been zero to one (as Table 7.2 shows).

During the 1950s the Diet passed a number of laws permitting "special industry" cartels. This legislation was usually worded in such a way as to exclude the JFTC from any role in approving the cartels. The power to allow the cartels was given to the specific government ministry involved, and the ministry was even given the power to coerce companies into joining the cartels. At one time the government did not hesitate to authorize this type of cartel. In 1966, for instance, there were 1,079 legally formed cartels in Japan. Only thirty of them were formed by JFTC approval as rationalization or recession cartels. All the rest were "special industry" cartels.[27]

In recent years, the number of authorized cartels has dropped rather steadily. In 1982, the amount was 505, as Table 7.2 shows. The fact that the number of cartels has diminished, however, does not mean that the importance of cartels is lessening in Japan. After all, the smaller number of cartels that now exist in Japan could conceivably

Table 7.1
An Overview of Fair Trade Commission Activity, FY 1947–1981

Type of Decision	1947	1948	1949	1950	1951	1952	1953	1954	1955	1956	1957	1958	1959	1960	1961	1962	1963	1964
Recommendation	0	0	2	4	4	3	5	0	5	5	7	2	2	1	3	7	24	30
Consent	5	2	11	45	6	4	5	2	1	0	0	0	0	0	0	5	11	0
Formal Decision	0	0	1	10	8	8	2	3	5	1	0	0	0	0	0	1	1	0
Court Appeal	0	0	0	1	0	1	1	1	1	0	0	1	2	0	0	0	0	0
Total	5	2	14	60	18	16	13	6	12	6	7	3	4	1	3	13	36	30

Type of Decision	1965	1966	1967	1968	1969	1970	1971	1972	1973	1974	1975	1976	1977	1978	1979	1980	1981
Recommendation	26	17	11	28	26	43	37	27	67	47	31	24	13	7	12	12	12
Consent	0	0	0	0	1	1	0	1	1	0	2	1	1	1	1	1	0
Formal Decision	1	0	1	3	5	0	0	6	1	13	1	0	4	0	2	3	1
Court Appeal	0	0	0	0	0	0	2	1	0	1	0	1	3	1	0	0	1
Total	27	17	12	31	32	44	39	35	69	61	34	26	21	9	15	16	14

Source: JFTC, *Kosei Torihiki Iinkai Nenji Hokoku* (Fair Trade Commission Annual Report), 1982.

Table 7.2
Authorized Cartels in Japan, 1953–1982
(number of cartels as of March 31 of each year)

	1953	1954	1955	1956	1957	1958	1959	1960	1961	1962	1963	1964	1965	1966	1967
Antimonopoly Act, Recession Cartels	—	0	0	0	1	1	5	4	3	0	1	2	2	16	1
Antimonopoly Act, Rationalization Cartels	—	0	0	4	6	6	8	9	9	11	11	14	14	14	13
Import-Export Trade Law, 1952–	0	6	14	37	71	93	150	172	193	199	202	202	210	214	210
Designated Electronics and Textiles Industry Rehabilitation Law, 1971–78	—	—	—	—	—	—	—	—	—	—	—	—	—	—	—
Medium-Small Industries Associations Law, 1953	53	71	143	194	218	280	314	370	467	549	591	588	587	652	634
Liquor Industry Law, 1953–	0	2	4	4	7	8	9	9	9	9	9	9	12	12	12
Sanitation Industry Law, 1957–	—	—	—	—	—	0	0	0	5	63	95	106	122	123	123
Fishery Export Industry Promotion Law, 1954–	—	—	0	8	8	11	10	11	10	11	11	11	12	11	8
Coastal Shipping Association Law, 1957–	—	—	—	—	—	1	9	10	12	13	16	15	14	16	21
Textile Industry Facilities Temporary Law, 1956–70	—	—	—	—	0	0	2	7	4	3	3	3	3	3	3
Depressed Industries Law, 1978–83	—	—	—	—	—	—	—	—	—	—	—	—	—	—	—
Other	0	0	1	1	1	1	2	3	2	10	12	20	23	18	15
Total	53	79	162	248	312	401	509	595	714	868	951	970	999	1,079	1,040

	1968	1969	1970	1971	1972	1973	1974	1975	1976	1977	1978	1979	1980	1981	1982
Antimonopoly Act, Recession Cartels	0	0	0	0	9	2	0	2	1	1	6	4	1	1	3
Antimonopoly Act, Rationalization Cartels	13	12	10	13	10	10	9	0	0	0	1	0	1	1	0
Import-Export Trade Law, 1952–	216	221	218	195	177	181	138	109	98	86	75	74	70	66	62
Designated Electronics and Textiles Industry Rehabilitation Law, 1971–78	—	—	—	0	0	13	15	17	16	15	9	—	—	—	—
Medium-Small Industries Associations Law, 1953	582	522	469	439	604	607	591	511	395	279	290	274	267	268	290
Liquor Industry Law, 1953–	12	10	7	7	7	4	4	0	0	0	0	0	0	0	0
Sanitation Industry Law, 1957–	123	123	123	123	123	123	122	122	122	122	122	122	122	122	122
Fishery Export Industry Promotion Law, 1954–	8	8	8	8	8	7	7	8	8	8	8	8	7	7	7
Coastal Shipping Association Law, 1957	22	22	22	21	19	14	7	4	4	5	5	5	5	5	6
Textile Industry Facilities Temporary Law, 1956–70	3	3	3	—	—	—	—	—	—	—	—	—	—	—	—
Depressed Industries Law, 1978–83	—	—	—	—	—	—	—	—	—	—	—	5	8	8	4
Other	24	33	26	39	19	18	15	15	10	12	18	14	10	11	15
Total	1,003	954	886	845	976	979	908	788	654	528	534	506	491	489	509

have more members or cover a greater amount of industrial output. One leading antitrust scholar in Japan has argued that the importance of cartels since 1977 has remained fairly constant since from that year to the present the ratio of manufacturing industry shipments covered by legal cartel arrangements to total manufacturing industry shipments has remained fairly constant.[28]

One rationale asserted by the Japanese as to why cartels are necessary is their belief that cooperative action among companies is beneficial to promote greater economic growth. Another, based on a Galbraithian countervailing power concept, is that small firms need to band together to bargain more equitably with larger domestic and foreign companies. The Japanese also asserted in their period of high growth that temporary recessions could force companies out of business despite a basically sound future outlook for the companies and their industry because of cash flow problems resulting from their high level of debt financing and relatively fixed labor costs. In the United States, of course, these arguments are not accepted: cartels are illegal per se.[29]

In 1978, the Diet passed a law to assist what were described as structurally depressed industries. That law provided a variety of measures, including coordinated cut-backs in production capacity, low-cost loans to facilitate the cutbacks, and legal cartels. Eventually fourteen industries cut back production capacity under the law. The law expired in June of 1983, and to replace it, MITI drew up legislation to provide assistance to eight industries.[30] At the time this book was being written, the legislation had been submitted to the Diet. If enacted, cartels formed to reduce capacity will again receive exemption from prosecution.

A crucial topic in discussing antitrust in Japan is administrative guidance. What happens when through administrative guidance a governmental agency such as MITI authorizes a collusive activity that violates the Antimonopoly Law? Before 1980, MITI's actions were without challenge, and the ministry seemed to be supreme in this area. The oil cartel criminal case of late 1980 may signify an end to MITI's dominance.[31]

Since the passage of the Petroleum Industry Act in 1962, the Japanese government and the petroleum refining industry have had a rather close relationship.[32] Under the statute, MITI was given a strong influence over many decisions of the industry, but the industry lacked any specific antitrust exemption. When in 1973 the Arab nations threatened to cut drastically the amount of oil they would sell to Japan, MITI agreed to an industry-proposed production cut, implemented afterward by the petroleum trade association. Concurrently, twelve of the oil refiners met to work out an agreement on price increases that was then approved by MITI.[33]

Attacking both the coordinated production cut and the price agreement, the JFTC took the unusual step of filing criminal charges at the Tokyo prosecutor's office rather than using its own administrative procedures. On September 26, 1980, the Tokyo High Court delivered its judgments.[34] The defendants were acquitted of charges stemming from the coordinated production cutback on the grounds that the industry action had been consistent with MITI's directions. The action itself was illegal, the court declared, but by carrying out MITI's wishes the companies showed no criminal intent. They could not, said the court, be held liable by one branch of the government (the JFTC) for doing what another branch (MITI) told them to do.

In a far more important part of the opinion, the Tokyo High Court excoriated MITI for its indiscriminate use of administrative guidance. The court declared that by encouraging and permitting the petroleum industry to carry out a coordinated production cut, MITI had subverted the very intention of the Antimonopoly Law. The court went on to find the twelve firms involved and their executives guilty of price-fixing. Although the defendants had received the blessing of MITI after the fact, they were not following specific administrative guidance or furthering MITI's policies. The argument of the oil companies and their executives that they were not liable because of MITI's approval of their actions was not sufficient justification, held the court.

The case is an extremely important one. For the first time, MITI's contention that administrative guidance is an unfettered power had been rebuffed by the courts. Nothing in the decision struck down MITI's use of administrative guidance to sanction an otherwise illegal activity, but what is important is that the decision strengthened the long-standing position of the JFTC in its bureaucratic battle against MITI that administrative guidance is not an acceptable excuse for illegal collusion.

The issue still outstanding after the oil cartel case is what the acceptable limits of administrative guidance in Japan are. Certainly, the decision imposes new risks on companies operating in Japan. The court did not hold all administrative guidance violative of the antitrust laws of Japan, nor did it indicate that such guidance would never exempt a firm from the antitrust laws. Yet, it did for the first time deny that administrative guidance would necessarily exempt a firm, and fourteen executives who had relied on such guidance were sentenced to prison. The case does indicate that a company facing an anticompetitive directive of MITI (or, indeed, any other governmental agency) will now need to make an independent assessment of the legality of its compliance. No longer can the enterprise simply rely on the ministry's assurances. Instead, if in obeying the directive it would violate the Antimonopoly Law, the company must make what is a distinctly unpleasant choice: obey MITI and risk the wrath of the JFTC and the courts, or avoid prosecution and incur the powerful unofficial sanctions of MITI. The state is set for the denouement of this intragovernmental struggle between MITI, a ministry which has never abandoned its philosophical attachment to the idea of governmental intervention to moderate "excessive competition," and the JFTC, the sole agency in Japan charged with enforcement of the antitrust laws.

NOTES

1. Rotwein, "Economic Concentration and Monopoly in Japan—A Second View," 36 *J. of Asian Studies* 57 (November 1976).

2. *See, e.g.*, Yoshio Kanazawa, "The Regulation of Corporate Enterprise: The Law of Unfair Competition and the Control of Monopoly Power," in *Law in Japan—The Legal Order in a Changing Society* 480, 482 (A. von Mehren ed. 1963) [hereinafter Kanazawa].

3. Edward Lincoln, "Antitrust Policy in Japan," *United States—Japan Trade Council Report No. 24*, August 10, 1979, at 1 [hereinafter Lincoln].

4. For an excellent discussion of SCAP's analysis of Japan's economy after World War II and the policies it favored, *see* E. Hadley, *Antitrust in Japan* (1970).

5. Law No. 54, April 14, 1947.

6. Kanazawa, *supra* note 2, at 485.

7. Law No. 54, Art. 1, April 14, 1947, as cited in II EHS KA2.

8. *Id.*, Art. 2 (6).

9. *Id.*, Art. 2 (9).

10. *Id.*, Art. 2 (9).

11. *Id.*, Art. 27 *et. seq.*

12. *Id.*, Art. 27 (2), 28. The JFTC is in fact the only independent regulatory agency still existing in Japan.

13. *Id.*, Art. 29, amended by Law No. 91 of 1947 and Law No. 257 of 1952.

14. *Id.*, Art. 85.

15. *Id.*, Art. 25, 26, 89 *et. seq.*

16. Pursuant to 15 U.S.C. § 15(a), victorious private plaintiffs in U.S. antitrust cases are entitled to three times the damages sustained.

17. Law No. 259, September 1, 1953.

18. C. Johnson, *MITI and the Japanese Miracle* 255-260 (1982).

19. *Japan v. Idemitsu Kosan, K.K.*, 985 Hanrei Jiho 3 (Tokyo High Ct., September 26, 1980) (hereinafter oil cartel case).

20. *See, e.g.*, Lincoln, *supra* note 3, at 3.

21. *See, e.g.*, Note, "Trustbusting in Japan: Cartels and Government—Business Cooperation," 94 *Harv. L. Rev.* 1064, 1076 (1981).

22. At least one defendant has argued that having the JFTC be both prosecutor and judge in this instance is wrong. That contention has been rejected by the Japanese courts. *Asahi Newspaper Co., Ltd., et. al. v. Fair Trade Commission* (Tokyo High Ct., March 9, 1953).

23. *See infra* note 14 and accompanying text.

24. J. Haley, "Antitrust Enforcement in Japan: Sleight-of-hand or Reality," *East Asian Executive Reports* 1 (July 15, 1980).

25. *See infra* note 8 and accompanying text.

26. Art. 24 (Law No. 259, September 1, 1953).

27. JFTC, *Kosei Torihiki Iinkai Nenji Hokuku* (Fair Trade Commission Annual Report) 358-362 (1978).

28. Mitsuo Matsushita, "The Antimonopoly Law of Japan," a paper presented at the Federal Bar Association U.S.-Japan Trade Law Conference, June 6-7, 1979.

29. 15 U.S.C. § 1.

30. Those industries are paper and pulp, ferroalloys, aluminum smelting, petrochemicals, fertilizer, polyvinyl chloride, open-hearth and electric furnace steel, and synthetic textiles. "Current Antitrust Policy in Japan," JEI Report No. 12A, April 1, 1983, at 6.

31. Oil cartel case, *supra* note 19.

32. Sekiyu gyo ho (Petroleum Industry Law) (Law No. 128 1962).

33. For a good analysis of the background of this case, *see* Ramseyer, "Japanese Antitrust Enforcement After the Oil Embargo," 31 *Am. J. Comp. L.* 395 (1983). For an excellent discussion of the oil cartel case and its significance, *see* 15 *Law in Japan: An Annual* 1-101 (1982).

34. 983 Hanrei jiho 22, 985 Hanrei jiho 3 (Tokyo High Ct., September 26, 1980).

Afterword

The incredible success of the Japan economic growth machine confronts us with enormous challenges—and enormous opportunity. Rather than publicly lambasting the Japanese for their "closed market," a tactic that often causes alienation but no perceptible result, we must seek to open further that incredibly potent market without rupturing relations with what has become one of our closest allies. Yet, at the same time we must learn from the Japanese example. Their business law system is still another example of how they have absorbed features from other systems that have worked and yet not abandoned indigenous traits. We must do the same. For too long, we have ignored features of foreign systems, smug in our belief that what works here will work there. Now, we have learned that such statements are not true. At the same time, however, we must not rush to adopt foreign traits to our system simply because these features have worked well for the Japanese. As I hope this book has shown, our people and cultures are very different, and many facets of one system will not transplant easily to the other.

What we must learn from the Japanese is that if we are to sell goods in their market, we must make an intelligent effort to understand them. Those who stay in Japan for any length of time are always amazed at how knowledgeable the people are concerning the United States and Americans (one reason for this knowledge is the pervasive coverage of the United States in the Japanese media). Japanese companies have combined this basic knowledge with an intense study of the American market to formulate an effective strategy to compete in the United States. Similarly, to find success in the marketplace of Japan, American companies must understand the country, its people, culture, and how they think. The Japanese market is obviously a lucrative one, and American companies must be determined to treat exports to it as a vital, ongoing part of their general sales and marketing strategy. Some parts of this strategy might include this advice:

—No longer treat exports as a stepchild. Too many U.S. companies think of exports as merely an incremental step of their business.

—Set export goals and stick to them, through good times and bad. Too many American companies consider exports an emergency sales outlet or a "dumping" place when domestic sales are poor.

—While developing export goals, don't jump with both feet into the Japanese market. Export sales success to Japan should not be expected overnight.

There is much talk today of how closed the Japanese market is to imports of American products. Blame is especially placed on the NTBs, the non-trade barriers. Yet many American firms are coping with these barriers and, after careful study of the Japanese market, have entered it profitably. Not only are fast-food chains, such as McDonald's, and American soft drinks found throughout Japan, but products from such companies as Schick, Proctor & Gamble, Kodak, IBM, Corning Glass, Xerox, Caterpillar, and Johnson & Johnson have large and profitable shares of the market. Despite all the talk of the difficulties inherent in U.S. companies entering the Japanese market, hundreds of U.S. firms have entered the Japanese market successfully. In total, more than 5,000 American companies send at least some exports to Japan.

The accomplishments in Japan of dozens of U.S. firms demonstrate that Japan is more open to imports than most Americans generally realize. American Express, for instance, has signed up nearly 100,000 customers in Japan for its prestigious Gold Card. CBS, through a 50-50 joint venture with Sony, has become the largest seller in Japan of phonograph records and prerecorded cassettes. Some American companies have even discovered the Japanese market to be more lucrative than the American one. Avon, for instance, which has stagnated in the United States in recent years, has more than 160,000 Japanese "Avon ladies" knocking on doors in a country where most married women still stay home during the day.

One of the themes of this book is how truly different the Japanese business law system is from ours. For an American to have a successful relationship with the Japanese, he must be cognizant of these differences. As complex as the Japanese language is, it is just one of those differences. Social customs and Japan's culture itself are two more. To have a successful business relationship with the Japanese, one must understand its business law system. The American's understanding, though, must go beyond that. Truly to understand this system, one must understand the history and culture—and, indeed, the ethos itself—of the Japanese people. The example of the many successful U.S. companies in Japan proves that this understanding, although difficult, can be achieved. The size of the Japanese market and its potential certainly make the attempt worthwhile.

Bibliography

GENERAL BIBLIOGRAPHIES

Association for Asian Studies, *Bibliography of Asian Studies* (Formerly *Far Eastern Bibliography, Annual*, from 1941-current). Published in Ann Arbor, Michigan.

Coleman, Rex, An Index to Japanese Law—A Bibliography of Western Language Materials 1867-1973, *Law in Japan: An Annual, Special Issue* (1975). Published in Tokyo, Japan.

Lee, Takika S., "Japanese Law: A Selective Bibliographical Guide," 63 *Law Library Journal* 189 (1970). Published in Chicago, Illinois.

Scheer, Matthias, "Index to Japanese Law," Supplement No. 5, 11 *Law in Japan: An Annual* 125 (1978). Published in Tokyo, Japan.

BOOKS

Abegglen, James, *The Japanese Factory: Aspects of Its Social Organization* (Glencoe, Ill., Free Press, 1958).

Adams, T.F.M. and Hoshii, Iwao, *A Financial History of the New Japan* (Tokyo, Kodansha Int., Ltd., 1972).

Akita, George, *Foundations of Constitutional Government in Modern Japan 1865-1900* (Cambridge, Harvard University Press, 1967).

Alan, G.C., *How Japan Competes: A Verdict on "Dumping"* (Lancing, W. Sussex, England, The Institute of Economic Affairs, 1978).

Austin, Lewis (ed.), *Japan: The Paradox of Progress* (New Haven, Yale University Press, 1976).

Ballon, Robert (ed.), *Marketing in Japan* (Tokyo, Sophia University & Kodansha Int., Ltd., 1974).

Beasley, W.G., *The Meiji Restoration* (Stanford, Stanford University Press, 1972).

———, *Modern Japan—Aspects of History, Literature and Society* (Rutland, Vt., Charles E. Tuttle Co., Inc., 1976).

Beckmann, George, *The Making of the Meiji Constitution* (Lawrence, University Press of Kansas, 1957).

———, *The Making of the Meiji Constitution: The Oligarchs and the*

Constitutional Development of Japan, 1868-1891 (Westport, Greenwood Press, 1975).

Benedict, Ruth, *The Chrysanthemum and the Sword* (Rutland, Vt., Charles E. Tuttle Co., 1946).

Bisson, Thomas, *Zaibatsu Dissolution in Japan* (Berkeley, University of California Press, 1954).

Blaker, Michael, *Japanese International Negotiating Style* (New York, Columbia University Press, 1977).

Borton, Hugh, *Japan's Modern Century: From Perry to 1970* (New York, Ronald Press, rev. ed., 1970).

Brown, Delmer, *Conciliation in Japanese Law* (Seattle, University of Washington Press, 1965).

Burks, Ardath, *Japan, Profile of a Postindustrial Power* (Boulder, Westview Press, 1981).

Campbell, Dennis (ed.), *Transnational Legal Practice* (The Netherlands, Kluwer, 1982).

Chamberlain, Basil, *Japanese Things* (Rutland, Vt., Charles E. Tuttle Co., 1971).

Christopher, Robert, *The Japanese Mind: The Goliath Explained* (New York, Linden Press, 1983).

Clark, Rodney, *The Japanese Company* (New Haven, Yale University Press, 1979).

Cohen, Herb, *You Can Negotiate Anything* (Secaucus, N.J., Lyle Stuart, 1981).

Condon, John, *Intercultural Encounters* (Tokyo, Simul Press, 1974).

Cook, Alice, *Public Employee Labor Relations in Japan: Three Aspects* (Ann Arbor, University of Michigan Press, 1971).

DeBecker, Eric, *A Survey of Some Japanese Tax Laws: A Practical Exposition of the Most Important Japanese Tax Laws* (Washington, D.C., University Publications of America, Inc., 1979).

DeBecker, Joseph, *The Principles and Practice of the Civil Code of Japan* (Washington, D.C., University Publications of America, Inc., 1979).

Dening, Walter, *Japan in Days of Yore* (London, Fine Books, 1976).

Denison, Edward F., *How Japan's Economy Grew So Fast: The Sources of Postwar Expansion* (Washington, D.C., The Brookings Institution, 1976).

Doi, Teruo, *Digest of Japanese Court Decisions in Trademarks and Unfair Competition Cases* (Tokyo, Radiopress, 1971).

———, *Patent and Know-How Licensing in Japan and the United States* (Seattle, University of Washington Press, 1977).

Ehrenzweig, A.A., *American-Japanese Private International Law* (Dobbs Ferry, N.Y., Oceana, 1964).

Feigenbaum, Edward A. and McCorduck, Pamela, *The Fifth Generation* (Reading, Mass., Addison-Wesley Publishing Co., 1983).

Gibney, Frank, *Japan: The Fragile Super Power* (New York, Signet, 1980).

Goedertier, Joseph M., *A Dictionary of Japanese History* (New York, John Weatherhill, Inc., 1968).

Gomi, Y., *Guide to Japanese Taxes 1980-81* (Tokyo, Zaikei Shoho-Sha, 1980).

Gray, Whitmore, *Current Studies in Japanese Law* (Ann Arbor, University of Michigan Press, 1979).

Gresser, Julian, *Environmental Law in Japan* (Cambridge, MIT Press, 1981).

Grossberg, Kenneth, *The Laws of the Muromachi Bakufu* (Tokyo, Sophia University, 1981).

Guillain, Robert, *The Japanese Challenge* (Philadelphia, J.B. Lippincott Co., 1970).

Hadley, Eleanor, *Antitrust in Japan* (Princeton, Princeton University Press, 1970).

Haley, John (ed.), *Current Legal Aspects of Doing Business in Japan and East Asia* (Seattle, American Bar Association, 1978).

Hall, John Carey, *Japanese Feudal Law* (Washington, D.C., University Publications of America, Inc., 1979).

Hall, John W. (ed.), *Studies in the Institutional History of Early Modern Japan* (Princeton, Princeton University Press, 1968).

Halloran, Richard, *Japan: Images and Realities* (Rutland, Vt., Charles E. Tuttle Co., 1970).

Hanami, T.A., *Labour Law and Industrial Relations in Japan* (The Netherlands, Kluwer, 1979).

Hane, Mikiso, *Japan: A Historical Survey* (New York, Charles Scribner's Sons, 1972).

Harrison, John A. (ed.), *Japan: Enduring Scholarship Selected From The Far Eastern Quarterly, The Journal of Asian Studies 1941-1971* (Tucson, The University of Arizona Press, 1972).

Hattori, Takaaki and Henderson, Dan, *Civil Procedure in Japan* (New York, Matthew Bender, 1983).

Henderson, Dan (ed.), *The Conciliation and Japanese Law: Tokugawa and Modern* (Seattle, University of Washington Press, 1965).

————, *The Constitution of Japan, Its First Twenty Years, 1947-67* (Seattle, University of Washington Press, 1968).

————, *Foreign Enterprise in Japan* (Rutland, Vt., Charles E. Tuttle Co., 1973).

Henderson, Dan, *Village Contracts in Tokugawa Japan* (Seattle, University of Washington Press, 1975).

Henderson, Dan and Haley, John, *Law & the Legal Process in Japan* (Seattle, University of Washington Press, 1978).

Hirschmeier, Johannes, *The Origins of Entrepreneurship in Meiji Japan* (Cambridge, Harvard University Press, 1964).

Hofheinz, Roy and Calder, Kent, *The Eastasia Edge* (New York, Basic Books, Inc., 1982).

Imai, Masaaki, *Never Take Yes For An Answer* (Tokyo, Simul Press, 1975).

Ishida, Eiichiro, *Japanese Culture; A Study of Origins and Characteristics* (Tokyo, University of Tokyo Press, 1974).

Ishimine, Keitetsu, *A Comparative Study of Judicial Review Under American and Japanese Constitutional Law* (Ann Arbor, University Microfilms International, 1974).

Ito, Hirobumi, *Commentaries on the Constitution of the Empire of Japan* (Westport, Greenwood Press, 2nd ed., 1978).

Itoh, Hiroshi and Beer, Lawrence (eds.), *The Constitutional Case Law of Japan: Selected Court Decisions, 1961-1970* (Seattle, University of Washington Press, 1978).

Iyori, J. Hiroshi, *Antimonopoly Legislation in Japan* (New York, Federal Legal Publication, 1969).

Japan Culture Institute (ed.), *A Hundred Things Japanese* (Tokyo, Japan Culture Institute, 1975).

Japan External Trade Organization (JETRO) (ed.), *How to Succeed In Japan: A Guide For The Foreign Businessman* (Tokyo, The Mainichi Newspapers, 1974).

Johnson, Chalmers, *Japan's Public Policy Companies* (Washington, D.C., American Enterprise Institute for Public Policy Research, 1978).

———, *MITI and the Japanese Miracle* (Stanford, Stanford University Press, 1982).

Kapoor, A., *Asian Business* (Princeton, Darwin Press, Inc., 1976).

Kershner, Thomas, *Japanese Foreign Trade* (Lexington, Mass., Lexington Books, 1975).

Kitagawa, Zentaro (ed.), *Doing Business in Japan* (New York, Matthew Bender, 1982).

Lincoln, Edward, and Rosenthal, Douglas (chairmen), *Legal Aspects of Doing Business in Japan 1983* (New York, Practising Law Institute, 1983).

Livingston, Jon, *Imperial Japan, 1800-1945* (New York, Pantheon Books, 1973).

———, *Postwar Japan* (New York, Pantheon Books, 1973).

Lockwood, William, *The Economic Development of Japan* (Princeton, Princeton University Press, 2nd ed., 1968).

——— (ed.), *The State and Economic Enterprise in Japan* (Princeton, Princeton University Press, 1965).

McKinsey and Company, Inc., *Japan Business, Obstacles and Opportunities* (Prepared for the United States, Japan Trade Study Group, United States Publisher John Wiley and Sons, Inc., 1983)

MacKnight, Susan, *Japan's Expanding Manufacturing Presence in the United States: A Profile* (Washington, D.C., Japan Economic Institute of America, 1981).

Maki, John M. (ed.), *Court and Constitution in Japan* (Seattle, University of Washington Press, 1964).

——— (ed.), *Japan's Commission on the Constitution: The Final Report* (Seattle, University of Washington Press, 1980).

Meyer, Milton, *Japan: A Concise History* (Totowa, N.J., Littlefield, Adams, 1976).

Minear, Richard, *Japanese Tradition and Western Law* (Cambridge, Harvard University Press, 1970).

Moore, Charles, *The Japanese Mind: Essentials of Japanese Philosophy and Culture* (Honolulu, East-West Center Books, 1975).

Nakamura, Kichisahuro, *The Formation of Modern Japan as Viewed From Legal History* (Tokyo, Kasai Publishing and Printing, 1964).

Nakane, Chie, *Japanese Society* (Berkeley, University of California Press, 1970).

Noda, Yosiyuki, *Introduction to Japanese Law* (Angelo trans., Tokyo, University of Tokyo Press, 1976).

Norbury, Paul and Bownas, Geoffrey (eds.), *Business in Japan: A Guide to Japanese Business Practice and Procedure* (London, Macmillan Press, Ltd., 1974).

Nunn, Godfrey, *Japanese Periodicals and Newspapers in Western Languages: An International Union List* (London, Monsell, 1979).

Ohta, Thaddeus Y., *Japanese National Government Publications in the Library of Congress: A Bibliography* (Washington, D.C., Library of Congress: U.S. Government Printing Office, 1981).

Ozaki, Robert, *The Control of Imports and Foreign Capital in Japan* (New York, Praeger, 1972).

Pascale, Richard, *The Art of Japanese Management* (New York, Warner Books, 1981).

Patrick, Hugh and Rosovsky, Henry (eds.), *Asia's New Giant: How the Japanese Economy Works* (Washington, D.C., The Brookings Institution, 1976).

Reischauer, Edwin O., *The Japanese* (Cambridge, Belknap Press, 1977).

——, *Japan: Tradition and Transformation* (Boston, Houghton Mifflin, 1978).

Saikaku, Ihara, *Tales of Japanese Justice* (Honolulu, University of Hawaii Press, 1980).

Sansom, George, *A History of Japan* (Stanford, Stanford University Press, 1958).

——, *Japan: A Short Cultural History* (London, The Current Press, 1952).

Sawada, J. Toshio, *Subsequent Conduct and Supervening Events* (Ann Arbor, University of Michigan Law School, 1968).

Schlesinger, R., *Comparative Law* (Mineola, N.Y., Foundation Press, 3rd ed., 1970).

Sebald, William Joseph, *Japan: Prospects, Options, and Opportunities* (Washington, D.C., American Enterprise Institute for Public Policy Research, 1967).

Seward, Jack, *America and Japan: The Twain Meet* (Tokyo, Lotus Press, 1981).

——, *Japanese in Action* (New York, John Weatherhill, Inc., 1968).

Shapiro, Isaac (chairman), *Legal Aspects of Doing Business with Japan* (New York, Practising Law Institute, 1981).

Shattuck, Warrenand Kitagawa, Zentaro, *United States-Japanese Contract and Sale Problems* (Seattle, University of Washington Press, 1973).

Smith, Thomas, *The Agrarian Origins of Modern Japan* (Stanford, Stanford University Press, 1959).

Smith, Warren, *Confucianism in Modern Japan* (Tokyo, The Hokuseido Press, 1959).

Tajima, Yoshiro, *How Goods Are Distributed in Japan* (Seward trans., Tokyo, Walton-Ridgeway and Co., 1971).

Tanaka, Hideo (ed.), *The Japanese Legal System* (Tokyo, University of Tokyo Press, 1976).

Tatsata, Misao, *Securities Regulation in Japan* (Tokyo, University of Tokyo Press, 1970).

Trager, J., *Letters from Sachiko* (New York, Atheneum, 1982).

Tsuneta Yano Memorial Society (ed.), *Nippon: A Charted Survey of Japan 1979/80* (Tokyo, Kokusei-sha, 1979).

Tsurumi, Y., *Sogoshosha—Engines of Export-Based Growth* (Montreal, Institute for Research on Public Policy, 1980).

Varley, Paul, *Japanese Culture: A Short History* (Rutland, Vt., Charles E. Tuttle Co., 1976)

Vogel, Ezra, *Japan as Number One: Lessons for America* (Cambridge, Harvard University Press, 1979).
——,*Modern Japanese Organization and Decisionmaking* (Berkeley, University of California Press, 1975).
Von Mehren, Arthur Taylor (ed.), *Law in Japan—The Legal Order in a Changing Society* (Cambridge, Harvard University Press, 1963).
——, and Gordley, James Russell, *The Civil Law System* (Boston, Little, Brown and Company, 2nd ed., 1977).
Wigmore, John Henry, *Law and Justice in Tokugawa Japan* (10 vols.) (Tokyo, University of Tokyo Press, 1971).
Woronoff, Jon, *Japan, the Coming Social Crisis* (Tokyo, Lotus Press, 1981).
Yamamura, Keozeo, *Economic Policy in Postwar Japan* (Berkeley, University of California Press, 1967).
Yoshihara, Kunio, *Japanese Investment in Southeast Asia* (Honolulu, University of Hawaii Press, 1978).
Yoshino, Michael Y., *Japan's Managerial System* (Cambridge, MIT Press, 1968).

PERIODICALS

Asian Law Journal (Asian Legal Research Institute, 1978-current).
Asian Studies Newsletter (Association for Asian Studies, Inc., November 1980-current).
Current Studies in Japanese Law (Center For Japanese Studies, University of Michigan, Occasional Papers).
The East (The East Publications, Inc., April/May 1964-current).
Far Eastern Economic Review (Far Eastern Economic Review, Ltd., 1946-current).
International Lawyer's Newsletter (International Lawyer's Newsletter, 1979-current).
The Japan Annual of Law and Politics (Second Division, Science Council of Japan, 1952-current).
The Japan Business Law Journal: A Monthly Interpretive Legal and Business Review of Japan for Business Leaders and Their Advisors (Sangyo Horei Center, Inc., 1980-current).
Japan Economic Institute Report (Japan Economic Institute, 1981-current).
The Japan Economic Journal (Nihon Keizai Shimbun, Inc., 1983).
The Japan Foundation Newsletter (Japan Foundation, Tokyo, Japan, vol. 4, 1976-current).
Japan Insight (United States-Japan Trade Council, January 1980-current).
The Japan Newsletter (Eagle Enterprises, Ltd., 1982).
The Japan Trade Law Bulletin (Japan Trade, 1982-current).
Japanese American Society for Legal Studies Reports, American Branch (1981-current).
The Japanese Annual of International Law (The Japan Branch of the International Law Association, 1957-current).
JASLS Reports—Newsletter of the Japanese American Society for Legal Studies, American Branch (1980-current).

The Journal of Asian Studies (The Association for Asian Studies, Inc., February 1981-current).

Journal of Japanese Studies (The Society for Japanese Studies, 1974-current).

Journal of Japanese Trade & Industry (Japan Economic Foundation, January 1982-current).

The International Lawyer (A Quarterly Publication of the Section of International Law/American Bar Association, 1966-current).

Law in Japan: An Annual (Japanese American Society for Legal Studies, 1967-current).

Pacific Basin Law Journal (University of California, Los Angeles, 1982-current).

Tradepia International (Nissho Iwai Corporation, 1982-current).

PUBLICATIONS

The American Society of International Law, *Japan's Assimilation of Western International Law* (Reprinted from the Proceedings of the 69th Annual Meeting of the American Society of International Law, April 1975).

Arthur D. Little, Inc., *The Japanese Non-Tariff Trade Barrier Issue: American Views and the Implications for Japan-U.S. Trade Relations* IV (1979).

Financial Commissioner's Office, Ministry of Finance, *Guide to Economic Law of Japan* (Washington, D.C., University Publications of America, Inc., 1979).

Institute of International Investment, *A Guide for Foreign Investors* (1964).

Japan Economic Institute, *Japan's Import Barriers: An Analysis of Divergent Bilateral Views* (1981).

Japan External Trade Organization (JETRO), *Business Information, Series 1-8* (disseminated by Japan Trade Center, New York, 1980).

Japan External Trade Organization (JETRO), *Marketing, Series 1-8* (disseminated by Japan Trade Center, New York, 1980).

Japan Fair Trade Commission, *Kosei Torihiki Iinkai Nenji Hokoku* (Fair Trade Commission Annual Report).

Japan Securities Research Institute, *Lectures on Japanese Securities Regulation* (1980).

Japan Special Libraries Association Directory of Information Sources in Japan, 1980 (Nichigai Associates, distributed by Kinokuniya Book-Store, 1979).

Kaplan, Eugene, *Japan: The Government-Business Relationship, A Guide for the American Businessman* (Washington, D.C., U.S. Bureau of International Commerce, U.S. Government Printing Office, 1972).

Mainichi Newspapers, *Japan Almanac 1976: A Comprehensive Handbook of Japan* (1976).

Ministry of Foreign Affairs, *Environmental Policy of Japan* (1977).

Ministry of Foreign Affairs of Japan, *100 Questions and Answers on Japan's Economy and Japan-U.S. Trade* (October 1978).

Ministry of International Trade and Industry Handbook (International Trade Policy Bureau, 1979).

U.S. Export Opportunities to Japan (Washington, D.C., U.S. Department of Commerce, 1978).

U.S.-Japan Trade Council: Yearbook of U.S. Japan Economic Relations (Japan Economic Institute, a yearly publication, 1978-current).

U.S.-Japan Trade Study Group: A Special Progress Report (U.S.-Japan Trade Study Group [TSG], 1980).

JAPANESE LAW MATERIALS

EHS Law Bulletin Series (Eibun-Horei-Sha, Inc., Tokyo, 1970-current).

Japan: Laws, Ordinances and Other Regulations Concerning Foreign Exchange and Foreign Trade (Chuo Shuppan Kikaku Co., 1982).

Ministry of Labor, *Japan Labor Code* (Washington, D.C., University Publications of America, Inc., 1979).

ARTICLES

Abe, Haruo, "Criminal Justice in Japan: Its Historical Background and Modern Problems," 47 *A.B.A.J.* 555 (1961).

Anderson, Andrew, "The Law Partially Amending the Foreign Trade Control Law," 1 *J.A.S.L.S. Reporter* 1 (1980).

Ariga, Michiko, "The Antimonopoly Law of Japan and Its Enforcement," 39 *Wash. L. Rev.* 437 (1964).

———, "International Trade of Japan and the Antimonopoly Act," 9 *J. Int'l L. and Econ.* 185 (1973).

———, "Merger Regulation in Japan," 5 *Tex. Int'l Law F.* 112 (1969).

Balassa, Bela, "The Tokyo Round and the Developing Countries," 14 *Journal of World Trade Law* 93 (1980).

Ballon, R.J., "Japan's Investments Overseas," 28 *Ausseauwirtschaft* 128 (1973).

Beer, Lawrence, "Defamation, Privacy and Freedom of Expression in Japan," 5 *Law in Japan: An Annual* 192 (1975).

———, "A Guide to the Study of Japanese Law," 23 *Am. J. Comp. L.* 284 (1975).

Birmingham, Hobart, "Japanese Postwar Attitudes Toward International Trade and Investment," 2 *Hastings Int'l and Comp. L. R.* 1 (1979).

Bix, Herbert, "Rethinking Emperor-System Fascism: Ruptures and Continuities in Modern Japanese History," 14 *Bulletin of Concerned Asian Scholars* 2 (1982).

Bolz, Herbert F., "Judicial Review in Japan," 4 *Hastings Int'l and Comp. L. R.* 87 (1980).

Book Review, "Japan's Technological Challenge to the West, 1950-1974: Motivation and Accomplishment" (Ozawa), 10 *Journal of World Trade Law* 305 (1976).

Brockman, Rosser, "Japanese Taxation of the Foreign Income of Japanese Corporations," 2 *Hastings Int'l and Comp. L. R.* 73 (1979).

Brown, Ronald, "Government Secrecy and the People's Right To Know In Japan: Implications of the Nishiyama Case," 10 *Law in Japan: An Annual* 112 (1977).

Cappiello, Thomas, "The Changing Role of Japan's General Traders," *Tradepia International* 12 (Autumn 1982).

Cates, Armel, "Some Effects of Economic War on Parties to International Contracts," 1 *I.C.L.F. Rev.* 131 (1980).

Coleman, Rex, "The Japanese and Korean Law of Secured Transactions," 2 *Hastings Int'l and Comp. L. R.* 21 (1979).

Covey, J. Amanda, "Vertical Restraints Under Japanese Law: The Antimonopoly Law Study Group Report," 14 *Law in Japan: An Annual* 49 (1981).

Doi, Teruo, "Review of Court Decisions in Cases Involving International Business Transactions and Related Matters," 2 *Japan Business Law Journal* 284 (1981).

Dziubla, Robert, "International Trading Companies, Building on the Japanese Model," 4 *Nw. J. Int'l Law & Bus.* 422 (1982).

Fujita, Yasuhiro, "Procedural Fairness to Foreign Litigants as Stressed by Japanese Courts," 12 *Int. Lawyer* 795 (1978).

George, B.J., "The Japanese Judicial System: Thirty Years of Transition," 12 *Loy. L.A.L. Rev.* 807 (1979).

Gresser, Julian, "The 1973 Japanese Law for the Compensation of Pollution-Related Health Damage: An Introductory Assessment," 5 *ELR* 50229 (1975).

Guitland, Stephen, "Negotiating and Administering an International Sales Contract with the Japanese," 8 *Int'l Law* 822 (1974).

Hahn, Elliott, "Negotiating with the Japanese," 2 *Calif. Lawyer* 20 (1982), reprinted in 14 *Case Western Res. J. of Int'l L.* 377 (1982).

———, "The Rights of Newspaper Reporters and the Public Welfare Standard in Japan," 11 *Cal. W. Int'l L.J.* 189 (1981).

Haley, John, "Marketing and Anti-trust in Japan," 2 *Hastings Int'l and Comp. L. R.* 51 (1979).

———, "The Myth of the Reluctant Litigant," 4 *Journal of Japanese Studies* 359 (Summer 1978).

———,"Sheathing the Sword of Justice in Japan: An Essay on Law without Sanctions," 8 *Journal of Japanese Studies* 265 (Summer 1982).

Henderson, Dan, "Contracts in Tokugawa Villages," 1 *Journal of Japanese Studies* 51 (1974).

———, "Japan: Economic Aspects of National Security and Its Impact on U.S. Security," 1 *Public Law Forum* 99 (1981).

———, "Japanese Judicial Review of Legislation: The First Twenty Years," 43 *Wash. L. Rev.* 1005 (1968).

———, "Japanese Law In English: Reflections on Translation," 6 *Journal of Japanese Studies* 117 (1980).

———, "The Role of Lawyers in U.S.-Japanese Business Transactions," 38 *Wash. L. Rev.* 1 (1963).

———, "Some Aspects of Tokugawa Law," 27 *Wash. L. Rev.* 85 (1952).

Hildebrand, James, "Antimonopoly Law of Japan—Potential Contract Violation Under Article 6," 6 *N.Y.U.J. Int'l Law and Pol.* 215 (1973).

———, "Establishing a Joint Venture Company in Japan: Legal Considerations," 6 *Case Western Res. J. of Int'l L.* 199 (1974).

Ishida, Takeshi, "Fundamental Human Rights and the Development of Legal Thought in Japan," 8 *Law in Japan: An Annual* 39 (1975).

Japan External Trade Organization (JETRO), "Business Information Service No. 6," 1 *The International Contract* 572 (1980).

Johnson, Mark S., "The Japanese Milieu and Its Relationship to Business," 13 *Amer. Bus. Law J.* 339 (1976).

Kahei, Rokumoto, "The Law Consciousness of the Japanese," *The Japan Foundation Newsletter* 5 (February/March 1982).

Kamata, Sadao, "The Atomic Bomb and the Citizens of Nagasaki," 14 *Bulletin of Concerned Asian Scholars* 38 (1982).

Kawamura, A., "A New Development in Japanese Antitrust Law: Its Application to International Transactions," 3 *Lawasia* 179 (1972).

Kawashima, Takeyoshi, "The Legal Consciousness of Contract in Japan," 7 *Law in Japan: An Annual* 1 (Stevens trans., 1974).

Kim, Chin, "A Lawyer's Guide to Overseas Trading and Investment: Sources in English," 7 *The Journal of International Law and Economics* 115 (1972).

———, "The So-Called Cocom Case," 4 *Journal of World Trade Law* 604 (1970).

Kobayashi, Noritake, "The Japanese Approach to Multinationalism," 10 *Journal of World Trade Law* 177 (1976).

Koen-Cohen, B.A., "The Doctrine of Good Faith in Japanese Contract Law," 4 *Lawasia* 177 (1974).

Kojima, Kiyoshi, "Hidden Trade Barriers in Japan," 7 *Journal of World Trade Law* 137 (1973).

Kosugi, Takeo, "Regulation of Practice by Foreign Lawyers," 27 *Amer. J. Comp. L.* 678 (1979).

Kumakura, Yoshio, "Trademark Registrability in Japan," 2 *Japan Business Law Journal* 218 (1981).

Kuribayashi, Tadao, "The New Ocean Regime and Japan," 11 *Ocean Development and International Law* 95 (1982).

McCormack, Gavan, "Nineteen-Thirties Japan: Fascism?" 14 *Bulletin of Concerned Asian Scholars* 20 (1982).

McMahon, Margaret, "Legal Education in Japan," 60 *A.B.A.J.* 1376 (1974).

Matsushita, Mitsuo, "Antimonopoly Law in Japan—Relating to International Business Transactions," 4 *Case Western Res. J. Int'l L.* 124 (1972).

———, "The Antimonopoly Law of Japan," 11 *Law in Japan: An Annual* 57 (1978).

———, "The Antimonopoly Act of Japan and International Transactions," 14 *Japan Am. Int'l L.* 1 (1970).

———, "Export Control and Export Cartels in Japan," 20 *Harvard Int'l L.J.* 103 (1979).

———, "International Cartels and Article VI of the Anti-Monopoly Law," 2 *Japan Business Law Journal* 189 (1981).

———, "Regulation of Sole Import Distributorship Agreements Under the Japanese Antimonopoly Act," 18 *Japan Am. Int'l L.* 66 (1974).

Mikazuki, Akira, "A Comparative Study of Judicial Systems," 3 *Law in Japan: An Annual* 1 (1969).

Miyaoka, Tsunejiro, "The Safeguard of Civil Liberty in Japan," 4 *A.B.A.J.* 604 (1918).

Monroe, Wilbur, "The Rise of Tokyo as an International Financial Center," 8 *Journal of World Trade Law* 655 (1974).

Mukai, Ken and Toshitani, Nobuyoshi, "The Progress and Problems of Compiling the Civil Code in the Early Meiji Era," 1 *Law in Japan: An Annual* 25 (1967).

Nagao, Ryuichi, "The Legal Philosophy of Tatsukichi Minobe," 5 *Law in Japan: An Annual* 165 (1972).

Nakamura, Y., "The Office of the Trade Ombudsman," *JEI Report* No. 13A, 1, 2 (April 8,1983).

Narita, Yoriaki, "Administrative Guidance," 2 *Law in Japan: An Annual* 45 (1968).

Nevins, Thomas, "Japanese Industrial and Labor Relations (3) Employment Policy Programs," 2 *Japan Business Law Journal* 199 (1981).

Noda, Yosiyuki, "Nihon-Jin no Seikaku to Sono Ho-kannen" ("The Character of the Japanese People and Their Conception of Law"), 140 *Misuzu* 2 (1971).

Ohara, Yoshio, "Legal Aspects of Japan's Foreign Trade," 1 *Journal of World Trade Law* 1 (1967).

Ohba, Masashige, "Recent Changes in the Foreign Exchange Control Law and the Law Concerning Foreign Investment in Japan," *The International Contract—Law and Finance Review 1980 Yearbook* 162 (1981).

Ohira, Kaname, "Admission to the Bar, Disbarment and Disqualification of Lawyers in Japan and the United States—A Comparative Study," 38 *Wash. L. Rev.* 22 (1963).

Olechowski, Andrzej, "Current Trade Restrictions in the EEC, the United States and Japan," 14 *Journal of World Trade Law* 220 (1980).

Ooya, Ken-ichi, "The Significance of Claim Drafting and Sufficient Disclosure in Japanese Patent Application and Infringement Procedure," 10 *I.L.C.* 573 (1979).

Ozawa, Terutomo, "Japan's New Resource Diplomacy: Government Backed Group Investment," 14 *Journal of World Trade Law* 3 (1980).

———, "Technology Imports and Direct Foreign Investment in Japan," 7 *Journal of World Trade Law* 666 (1973).

Pascale, Richard and Rohlen, Thomas, "The Mazda Turnaround," 9 *Journal of Japanese Studies* 219 (Summer 1983).

Ramseyer, J, Mark, "Japanese Antitrust Enforcement After the Oil Embargo," 31 *Am. J. Comp. L.* 395 (1983).

Rotwein, Eugene, "Economic Concentration and Monopoly in Japan—A Second View," 36 *J. of Asian Studies* 57 (November 1976).

Salwin, Lester, "The New Commercial Code of Japan: Symbol of Gradual Progress Toward Democratic Goals," 50 *Georgetown L.J.* 478 (1962).

Sanekata, Kenji, "Administrative Guidelines and the Antimonopoly Laws," 10 *Law in Japan: An Annual* 65 (1977).

Smith, Malcom D.H., "Prices and Petroleum in Japan 1973-74: A Study of Administrative Guidance," 10 *Law in Japan: An Annual* 81 (1977).

Stevens, Charles, "Japanese Law and the Japanese Legal System: Perspectives for the American Business Lawyer," 27 *Business Lawyer* 1259 (July 1972).

Tanaka, Hideo, "The Appointment of Supreme Court Justices and the Popular Review of Appointments," 11 *Law in Japan: An Annual* 25 (1978).

——— "The Role of Private Persons in the Enforcement of Law: A Comparative

Study of Japanese and American Law," 7 *Law in Japan: An Annual* 34 (1974).

Taniguchi, Yasuhei, "Litigious and Non-Litigious Dispute Settlement—Japanese Civil Justice: An Introduction" 2 *Japan Business Law Journal* 208 (1981).

Tatsuta, Misao, "Enforcement of Japanese Securities Legislation," 1 *J. of Comp. Corp. Law and Sec. Reg.* 95 (1978).

——, "Restrictions on Foreign Investment: Developments in Japanese Law," 3 *J. of Comp. Corp. Law and Sec. Reg.* 159 (1981).

Tharp, David, "Fractured Japanese," *The Japan Times*, June 14, 1980.

Tsuji, Yoshihiko, "Regulation of Resale Price Maintenance in Japan," 18 *N.Y.L. Forum* 397 (1972).

Tsurumi, Yoshi, "Japanese Multinational Firms," 7 *Journal of World Trade Law* 74 (1973).

Ukai, Nobushige, "The Individual and the Rule of Law Under the New Japanese Constitution," 51 *Nw. U. L. Rev.* 733 (1957).

Upham, Frank, "Litigation and Moral Consciousness in Japan, An Interpretive Analysis of Four Japanese Pollution Suits," 10 *Law and Society Rev.* 579 (1976).

Vaughn, Francis, "Introduction to Joint Venturing in Japan," 6 *Case Western Res. J. of Int'l L.* 178 (1974).

Ward, Robert, "The Origins of the Present Japanese Constitution," 50 *Am. Pol. Sci. Rev.* 980 (1956).

Watanabe, Osamu, "E.T. Too Brutal," *Journal of Japanese Trade and Industry* 5 (September 1982).

Weil, Frank, "Japan—Is the Market Open? A View of the Japanese Market Drawn From U.S. Corporate Experience," 11 *Law and Pol. in Int'l Bus.* 845 (1979).

Yamanouchi, Kazuo, "Administrative Guidance and the Role of Law," 7 *Law in Japan: An Annual* 22 (1974).

Yamashita, H. Dick, "The Stakes and the Statistics," 2 *Journal of Japanese Trade and Industry* 23 (March/April 1983).

Yamauchi, K., "About the Cocom Decision," 434 *Jurisuto* (Jurist) 71 (1969).

Notes and Comments

Note, "The Chips Are Down: Legal Implications of Alleged Japanese Unfair Practices in the United States Semiconductor Industry," 2 *Hastings Int'l and Comp. L. R.* 129 (1979).

Note, "Computer Technology Trade Secrets: Protection in an International Setting," 2 *Hastings Int'l and Comp. L. R.* 181 (1979).

Comment, "Designs on Sunshine: Solar Access in the United States and Japan," 10 *Conn. L. R.* 123 (1977).

Note, "European Court: Dumping of Japanese Bearings," 13 *Journal of World Trade Law* 361 (1976).

Note, "GATT: A Legal Guide to the Tokyo Round," 13 *Journal of World Trade Law* 436 (1976).

Comment, "Guide to International Trade and Investment Law in Japan," 9 *Journal of World Trade Law* 119 (1975).

Note, "Indexes of Selected Bilateral Treaties: United States and Japan," 2 *Hastings Int'l and Comp. L. R.* 105 (1979).

Note, "Individual Civil Liberties and the Japanese Constitution," 14 *Tulsa L.J.* 515 (1979).

Note, "Japanese Family Law," 9 *Stanford Law Review* 132 (1956).

Note, "Japanese Regulation of Technology Imports," 15 *Journal of World Trade Law* 83 (1981).

Comment, "Letting Obsolete Firms Die: Trade Adjustment Assistance in the United States and Japan," 22 *Harvard Int'l L.J.* 595 (1981).

Comment, "A New Development in Japanese Antitrust Law: Its Application to International Transactions," 3 *Law in Asia* 179 (1972).

Note, "Sogo Shoshas and Japan's Foreign Economic Relations," 13 *Journal of World Trade Law* 257 (1979).

Note, "Trustbusting in Japan: Cartels and Government—Business Cooperation," 94 *Harv. L. Rev.* 1064 (1981).

Index

About the Author

ELLIOTT J. HAHN is Associate Professor of Law at California Western School of Law, San Diego, and has taught at the University of Tokyo as part of the Santa Clara Summer in Tokyo Program and other Japanese universities. His special field of expertise is trade relations between the United States and Asia. His articles have appeared in *Northwestern Journal of International Law & Business, California Lawyer,* and *Case Western Reserve Journal of International Law.*